The Constitution of the United States

A Look at the Bill of Rights

Protecting the Rights of Americans

Amy Graham

MyReportLinks.com Books

an imprint of

Enslow Publishers, Inc.

Box 398, 40 Industrial Road
Berkeley Heights, NJ 07922
USA

MyReportLinks.com Books, an imprint of Enslow Publishers, Inc. MyReportLinks®
is a registered trademark of Enslow Publishers, Inc.

Library of Congress Cataloging-in-Publication Data

Graham, Amy.
  A look at the Bill of Rights : protecting the rights of Americans / Amy Graham.
      p. cm. — (Constitution of the United States)
  Includes bibliographical references and index.
  ISBN-13: 978-1-59845-064-4 (hardcover : alk. paper)
  ISBN-10: 1-59845-064-6 (hardcover : alk. paper)
    1. United States. Constitution. 1st-10th Amendments—Juvenile literature.   2. Civil rights—United
States—Juvenile literature. I. Title.
KF4750.G68 2008
342.7308'5—dc22
                                        2006033894

Printed in the United States of America

10 9 8 7 6 5 4 3 2 1

To Our Readers:
Through the purchase of this book, you and your library gain access to the Report Links that specifically
back up this book.
The Publisher will provide access to the Report Links that back up this book and will keep these Report
Links up to date on **www.myreportlinks.com** for five years from the book's first publication date.
We have done our best to make sure all Internet addresses in this book were active and appropriate when
we went to press. However, the author and the Publisher have no control over, and assume no liability
for, the material available on those Internet sites or on other Web sites they may link to.
The usage of the MyReportLinks.com Books Web site is subject to the terms and conditions stated on the
Usage Policy Statement on **www.myreportlinks.com**.
A password may be required to access the Report Links that back up this book. The password is found
on the bottom of page 4 of this book.
Any comments or suggestions can be sent by e-mail to comments@myreportlinks.com or to the address
on the back cover.

CONTENTS

About MyReportLinks.com Books   4

Time Line   5

1 THE SACRED RIGHTS OF HUMANITY   7

2 AMERICA: LAND OF THE FREE   22

3 UNDERSTANDING THE
    BILL OF RIGHTS   41

4 DEFENDING FREEDOM—THE
    BILL OF RIGHTS AT WORK   59

5 THE SUPREME COURT
    UPHOLDS THE CONSTITUTION   78

6 LIVING IN AMERICA: RECENT DEBATE
    ABOUT THE BILL OF RIGHTS   93

The Constitution of the United States   108

Report Links   116

Glossary   118

Chapter Notes   120

Further Reading   125

Index   126

MyReportLinks.com Books
Great Books, Great Links, Great for Research!

The Internet sites featured in this book can save you hours of research time. These Internet sites—we call them **"Report Links"**—are constantly changing, but we keep them up to date on our Web site.

When you see this "Approved Web Site" logo, you will know that we are directing you to a great Internet site that will help you with your research.

Give it a try! Type http://www.myreportlinks.com into your browser, click on the series title and enter the password, then click on the book title, and scroll down to the Report Links listed for this book.

The Report Links will bring you to great source documents, photographs, and illustrations. MyReportLinks.com Books save you time, feature Report Links that are kept up to date, and make report writing easier than ever! A complete listing of the Report Links can be found on pages 116–117 at the back of the book.

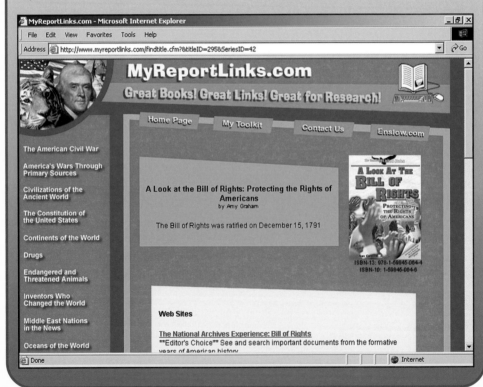

Please see "To Our Readers" on the copyright page for important information about this book, the MyReportLinks.com Web site, and the Report Links that back up this book.

Please enter **BRC1957** if asked for a password.

TIME LINE

1215 – King John of England signs the Magna Carta.

1620 – Puritans leave England in search of religious freedom.

1689 – England adopts a bill of rights.

1751 – James Madison is born in Virginia.

1776 – Thomas Jefferson writes the Declaration of Independence.

1776 – Second Continental Congress tells colonies to set up state governments.

1776 – George Mason writes the Virginia Declaration of Rights.

1781 – The states form a weak union under the Articles of Confederation.

1787 – Founding Fathers write the U.S. Constitution in Philadelphia.

1787 –1789 – Thomas Jefferson and James Madison correspond about a bill of rights.

1787 – George Mason publishes his Objections to the Constitution.

1788 – *The Federalist Papers,* supporting the Constitution, are published.

– The states ratify the Constitution; many suggest adding a bill of rights.

1789 – President Washington asks first Congress to address a bill of rights issue.

– Madison introduces a bill of rights to Congress.

– Congress suggests amending the Constitution to include a bill of rights.

1791 – The states ratify the Bill of Rights; it is added to the Constitution.

1868 – Fourteenth Amendment is passed. It would eventually extend most of the Bill of Rights to the states.

1917 – America declares war against Germany, entering World War I.

TIME LINE (CONT.)

- Congress passes the Espionage Act, making it illegal to criticize the war.

1919 – Supreme Court upholds the Espionage Act in *Schenck v. United States*.

1921 – Congress repeals the Sedition Act, an amendment to the Espionage Act.

1939 – Supreme Court rules that some gun control laws are legal.

1956 – Congress chooses "In God We Trust" as the nation's official motto.

1962 – Supreme Court rules government cannot write prayers.

1963 – Supreme Court stops public schools from having group prayers and Bible readings, but allows students to pray on their own.

1967 – Supreme Court strikes down a state law against interracial marriage.

1969 – Supreme Court rules that public-school students have a right to free speech.

1972 – Supreme Court says the death penalty is "cruel and unusual."

1976 – Death penalty is reinstated under new, fairer laws.

1989 – Supreme Court says burning the United States flag is protected as free speech.

- Congress passes the federal Flag Protection Act, outlawing flag burning.

1990 – Supreme Court strikes down the federal Flag Protection Act.

1995 – Supreme Court strikes down the Gun-Free School Zones Act.

2006 – Latest attempt at a Flag Protection Amendment dies in the Senate.

THE SACRED RIGHTS OF HUMANITY

1

o people have the right to be free? Do people have the right to think their own thoughts? Do they have the right to speak up for what they believe in? In the seventeenth century, these questions began a new way of thinking. Philosophers are people who study the world of ideas. They argued that people are born with certain rights. They said that these rights are fundamental. In other words, they are a part of being human. They argued that people have the right to free thought. They have the right to their own religious beliefs.[1] Today, most people agree with these ideas. Indeed, they are the foundation upon which the American government is built.

→ FREEDOM IS THE LAW: THE BILL OF RIGHTS

People may have the right to be free, but who guarantees their freedom? Thanks to the founders who set up the government, freedom is the law of the land in America. The founders agreed upon a list of

By adding the Bill of Rights to the Constitution, lawmakers ensured that the basic human rights of United States citizens could not legally be violated.

important human rights. They called it the Bill of Rights. They made these rights into law by adding them to the Constitution. The Bill of Rights became the first ten amendments to the Constitution. The Constitution has been in force for over two hundred years. Although a lot has changed in that time, the Bill of Rights continues to protect essential freedoms. It safeguards the rights of Americans. What would life be like without the Bill of Rights?

Everyone in the United States is born with the right to be free. Yet millions of people around the world never experience freedom. Their governments limit the rights of their citizens. Here are some examples from around the globe.

→FREEDOM TO SPEAK OUT AGAINST THE GOVERNMENT

What if you could be thrown in jail for something you wrote? Would you dare to speak up for the truth? According to a group called Reporters Without Borders, this is a question many writers must ask themselves. Reporters Without Borders works to support freedom of speech around the globe. They believe that people have the right to speak and write the truth. Each year, the group compiles a list of countries based on the freedom of their press. In 2005, they rated Iran one of the worst in the world.[2]

Reporters Without Borders serves as a "freedom of the press agency." Its Web site features news and press releases describing worldwide efforts to fight censorship and attacks on journalists by their governments.

Access this Web site from http://www.myreportlinks.com

Iran is a country in the Middle East. Iran's government is not a democracy. The country is not governed by the people. Instead, a small group of conservative Muslim holy men called mullahs rule Iran. Most of the people in Iran are Muslim. That does not mean they all agree with the government. It is a hard place to live if you disagree with the rulers. It is very dangerous to speak your mind. Journalists there live in fear. If they dare to speak out against the government, they take a big risk. They could face beatings, high fines, prison, torture, and even death.

One example was Akbar Ganji. He got out of jail in the spring of 2006 after having been held in prison for six years. What was his crime? Ganji is a reporter. His job was to write stories for daily newspapers. One article he wrote got him into deep trouble. It angered some powerful people. They held high posts in the government. They were mad because Ganji's article linked their names with a series of murders. The murder victims had spoken out for government reform. The government did not want them to talk. It had them killed. Ganji was brave to write the story.

Ganji became known around the world. He is a leading spokesperson for reform in Iran. He flew to Berlin to speak at a conference. People discussed how Iran could change for the better. When Ganji came back to Iran, the police arrested him. They accused him of "insulting the founder of the Islamic Republic and the regime's sacred values."[3] A court sentenced him to ten years in jail. After he served his sentence, he would have to live in exile, that is, away from the place he called home. He would not be able to return to his country for five years.

Ganji appealed his case. His sentence was reduced to six months. But Iran's supreme court stepped in. They quickly overrode the appeal. They sentenced him to six years in prison. Ganji suffered in jail. Prison guards tortured him. They demanded that he take back what he had written. He refused. They put him in a cell by himself. To protest, he went on a hunger strike. He did not eat food for sixty days. He lost a lot of weight—fifty-five pounds (twenty-five kilograms). Still, Ganji found ways to speak his mind. He wrote letters which were smuggled out of jail. People posted them on the Internet. People all over the world heard about Akbar Ganji. President George W. Bush asked the Iranian government to release Ganji.[4] They let him go a few weeks before he had served his full prison term. As of March 2006, Ganji is free. He is very weak and sick from his time in prison.

→ DEATH TO CONVERTS

What if you could be sentenced to death because of what you believe? For some people, this is a

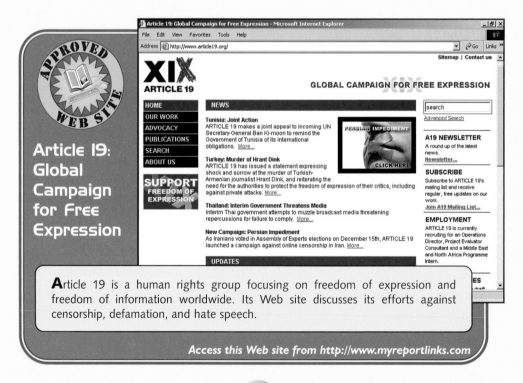

Article 19:
Global
Campaign
for Free
Expression

Article 19 is a human rights group focusing on freedom of expression and freedom of information worldwide. Its Web site discusses its efforts against censorship, defamation, and hate speech.

Access this Web site from http://www.myreportlinks.com

very real fear. It is for people in the country of Afghanistan. Islam is the national religion. It is against the law for people to convert from Islam. In 2001, the United States and Great Britain sent soldiers to Afghanistan. Their armies helped to free the country. They overthrew the Taliban, which was a group of conservative religious men who were in control of the country. Now Afghanistan is much more democratic than it was under the Taliban. Yet in 2006, a man was arrested because he had a Christian Bible. The man's name was Abdul Rahman. What exactly was his crime? He became a Christian sixteen years ago. If a court found him guilty, Rahman could be put to death.

People around the world were shocked and angry. The Afghans had just written a new constitution. Their new government was supposed to be a democracy. How could a democracy put someone to death for his or her beliefs?[5] It did not make sense. The court avoided ruling on the case by finding Rahman was not fit to stand trial. The court found he had a mental illness so they let him go. As soon as he was freed, Rahman fled to Italy and changed his name. He vowed never to return to his homeland. But the problem is not solved. What will happen to other converts in Afghanistan? One expert guesses that there are as many as ten thousand Christian converts living in Afghanistan today.[6] Perhaps they are at risk, too.

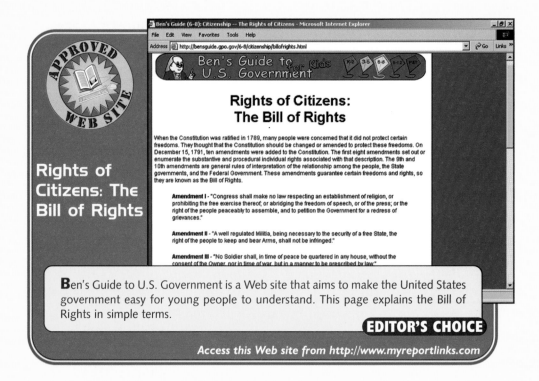

Rights of Citizens: The Bill of Rights

Ben's Guide to U.S. Government is a Web site that aims to make the United States government easy for young people to understand. This page explains the Bill of Rights in simple terms.

EDITOR'S CHOICE

Access this Web site from http://www.myreportlinks.com

→STUDENT JAILED FOR WEB SITE

What if the police could lock you up because of a few messages you posted on the Internet? This is happening more and more in Iran. Many young people have turned to the Internet. There they can voice their thoughts on blogs. Bloggers are people who post their ideas on a Web site. They keep a diary online for many to read. With the push of a button, their opinions are on the Internet for all to read. It is hard for any government to censor the Internet. The police do shut down Web sites. Yet new Web sites pop up instantly to take their place.

The leaders of Iran try to silence people through fear. They arrest bloggers and put them in jail, treating them like criminals. This is the fate of a young man named Mojtaba Saminejad. He is a college student who kept a Web log. In the fall of 2004, the Iranian police arrested some bloggers. They had spoken out against the government. Saminejad thought this was wrong. He said so on his Web log. The police came for him in November. The authorities released him several months later. When he could not pay the high bail, they put him back in prison. Human Rights Watch is an organization that exposes human rights violations. They

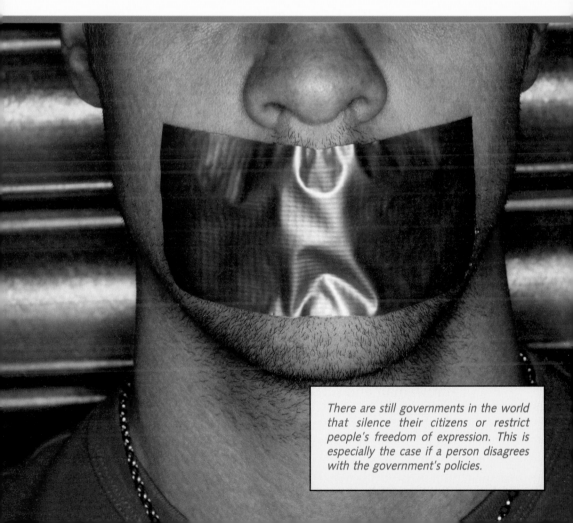

There are still governments in the world that silence their citizens or restrict people's freedom of expression. This is especially the case if a person disagrees with the government's policies.

are keeping an eye on this case. They report that, while in jail, Saminejad has been kept in a cell all by himself for eighty-eight days. The guards have beaten and tortured him.[7] As of June 2006, he is still in prison. The police did allow him to take his school exams. They led him to the exams in hand-cuffs. He was returned to his prison cell after the tests were over.[8] He faces a two year and ten month prison sentence.

➡ A GOVERNMENT THAT RULES BY FORCE

What if you lived in a place where the government ignored the will of the people? What if the people in charge ruled through brute force? This is true in Burma, a small country in Asia. (Some people call it by the name Myanmar, which is its official name.) A small group of military men is in control of the government. They use an army to make the citizens obey them. Many people in Burma are unhappy. They want a government that will represent them, not bully them. The largest group of reformers is the National League of Democracy. Their leader is a heroic woman by the name of Aung San Suu Kyi.

Suu Kyi was born in Burma, but she lived outside of her country for many years. She married a British man and settled in England. She came back to Burma to care for her elderly mother. She came back during a time of great change. People were

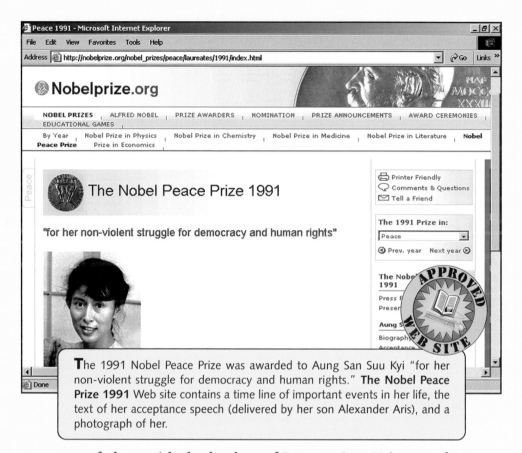

Peace 1991 - Microsoft Internet Explorer

File   Edit   View   Favorites   Tools   Help

Address http://nobelprize.org/nobel_prizes/peace/laureates/1991/index.html   Go   Links »

Nobelprize.org

NOBEL PRIZES   ALFRED NOBEL   PRIZE AWARDERS   NOMINATION   PRIZE ANNOUNCEMENTS   AWARD CEREMONIES
EDUCATIONAL GAMES

By Year   Nobel Prize in Physics   Nobel Prize in Chemistry   Nobel Prize in Medicine   Nobel Prize in Literature   **Nobel**
Peace Prize   Prize in Economics

The Nobel Peace Prize 1991

Printer Friendly
Comments & Questions
Tell a Friend

"for her non-violent struggle for democracy and human rights"

The 1991 Prize in:
Peace
Prev. year   Next year

The 1991 Nobel Peace Prize was awarded to Aung San Suu Kyi "for her non-violent struggle for democracy and human rights." **The Nobel Peace Prize 1991** Web site contains a time line of important events in her life, the text of her acceptance speech (delivered by her son Alexander Aris), and a photograph of her.

fed up with the leaders of Burma. Suu Kyi wanted to see democracy in her homeland. She ran for president of Burma in 1990. The military leaders were afraid. They feared that they would lose. They arrested Suu Kyi. They made her a prisoner in her own house. They would not allow her to see anybody, not even her family. They did not allow her to run for president. They took her name off the ballot, but people still voted for her. Suu Kyi's party won 82 percent of the vote. The government did not listen. The leaders did not step down. They are still in power today.[9]

Suu Kyi has not given up. She has pledged her life to work for democracy in Burma. Her courage has impressed people from all over the world. In 1991, Suu Kyi won the Nobel Peace Prize, given once a year to the person who struggled most for peace among peoples. She could not go to the award ceremony in Norway. She was still under house arrest. Her son and her husband went in her place and accepted the award for her. After six years, Suu Kyi was freed in 1995. She did not dare to leave Burma. Even when her husband was dying of cancer in England, she felt she could not

The White House: James Madison Web page is a biography of James Madison, the fourth president. In addition to serving as president, Madison drafted the text of the Bill of Rights. The page also shows a portrait of Madison and has links to other presidential biographies.

leave. He asked if he could visit her one last time. The Burmese government refused him. They said Suu Kyi could leave Burma to see him instead. She did not go. She was afraid she would not be allowed to come back. Suu Kyi's husband died in 1999 without a chance to say good-bye to her.

In May 2003, Suu Kyi and her party were ambushed on a country road. Government supporters planned the attack. As the sun went down, thousands of men jumped out of the woods. They carried rocks and sticks. The brutal attack went on into the night. Suu Kyi was hurt. According to one report, as many as seventy people may have been killed.[10] People talk about that day as Black Friday. Suu Kyi was put under house arrest once again. She is a symbol of hope for many. She is brave, despite the way she is treated. In the West, musicians wanted to help. They put together an album. It is called *For the Lady: Dedicated to Freeing Aung San Suu Kyi.* It includes the music of such stars as U2, Sting, Paul McCartney, Eric Clapton, and Coldplay. All of the money earned goes to help the cause of democracy in Burma.[11]

UPHOLDING THE BILL OF RIGHTS: THE DUTY OF ALL AMERICANS

People who live in the United States enjoy many freedoms. The Bill of Rights protects the freedoms of Americans. Early Americans fought for their independence from Great Britain. They wanted to be sure their new government would protect and serve them, not stifle them as the British had. By putting the Bill of Rights into the Constitution, they made sure America would be free for years to come. But the Bill of Rights is only a document. James Madison once called it a "parchment barrier."[12] He knew that any document is just a piece of paper. It is only as powerful as the people who stand up for it. Madison is one to listen to. People often call him the Father of the Bill of Rights. It

▲ The Supreme Court in 2007. Seated left to right are Anthony M. Kennedy, John Paul Stevens, Chief Justice John G. Roberts, Jr., Antonin Scalia, and David H. Souter. Standing left to right are Stephen G. Breyer, Clarence Thomas, Ruth Bader Ginsburg, and Samuel Alito, Jr.

was Madison who first introduced a bill of rights to Congress.

It is the job of the Supreme Court to make sure that the Bill of Rights is respected. The Supreme Court is the highest court in the United States. Its rulings decide how the law will be interpreted. Who serves on the Supreme Court? There are nine people. Each one is a highly experienced judge. When there is an open seat, the president chooses a justice to serve on the Supreme Court. The Senate must approve of the new judge. A Supreme Court justice can remain on the Court for the rest of his or her entire career. Citizens do not vote for Supreme Court justices. However, they do have a say. They indirectly elect the president (the Electoral College actually chooses the president) and directly elect the members of Congress. Through the people they elect, citizens can voice their opinions.

The Supreme Court has the job of enforcing the Bill of Rights. Yet it is too important to be left to a select few. That is why it is the duty of all Americans to stand up for what is right. Everyone should know what the Bill of Rights is and how it protects him or her. Only then can the Bill of Rights be more than just a paper barrier.

AMERICA: LAND OF THE FREE

Every year, on the fourth day of July, Americans celebrate. They march in parades and watch fireworks pop and whiz through the night sky. What is all the hoopla about? It is a birthday party, of sorts. It was on that day in 1776 that Americans broke free from England. They did this by issuing the Declaration of Independence. This document stated, "All men are created equal . . . endowed by their Creator with certain unalienable rights."[1] It proclaimed that their rights were being trampled upon by the British. They would no longer obey the king. They would rule themselves. The United States of America was born.

→ AMERICAN COLONIES: BEFORE THE REVOLUTION

What was life like in America back then? Why did Americans want to be free from Great Britain? The states were not yet recognized as states. They were British colonies, and they were under the rule of the British. There were thirteen colonies in all. In the north were Massachusetts, New Hampshire, Connecticut, and Rhode Island. In the south were Virginia, North Carolina, South Carolina, and Georgia. The colonies of New York, New Jersey, Delaware, Maryland, and Pennsylvania lay in the middle. Most of the people who lived in the colonies had come from Great Britain. They had come to make a life for themselves in the New World. The Old World was too crowded. There was not enough land. People came in search of their own land to farm. Some came to find a place where they could be free to be themselves. People in the Old World were often not tolerant of others. They were afraid of anyone who believed in a religion different from their own. They made laws to punish those who practiced another faith. They put them in jail. They even put them to death in some cases.[2]

→ WARS TO CONTROL THE NEW WORLD

The British were not alone in the New World. Before they came, tribes of American Indians lived on the land. People also crossed the sea from other places such as France and Spain. England, with its powerful navy, proved to be the mightiest. By 1763, the British had won control of the American colonies. Yet the wars had cost a lot of money. The British felt the colonists should help pay. The

The Pilgrims had come to North America from Great Britain to escape religious persecution. In America, they hoped to freely practice their religion.

British passed the Stamp Act and, later, the Tea Act. These acts forced the colonists to pay money to Great Britain. The colonists did not think the taxes were fair. They did not have any say in the British government. They had no seats in the British Parliament. "No taxation without representation!" they cried in protest. Americans believed they had the same rights as British citizens. That meant they should have the right to petition their king when they were unhappy. They wrote to King Henry V. They asked him to listen to them and address their concerns. Yet he ignored them.

THE REVOLUTIONARY WAR

The colonists grew angry. They felt bold. Great Britain was far away, and there was a great wide ocean between them. Who was going to make them pay? The British sent troops to enforce the law. This made the colonists even more upset. They wanted to be heard, not silenced! There were no barracks for the soldiers to live in. So the British put the soldiers in the homes of Americans. Americans had to give room and board to the army that was there to quiet them. It was like rubbing salt in a fresh wound. When the colonists met to complain, the British troops forced them to disband. They did not allow people to gather to criticize the government. The situation reached a boiling point. In April 1775, the first shots were

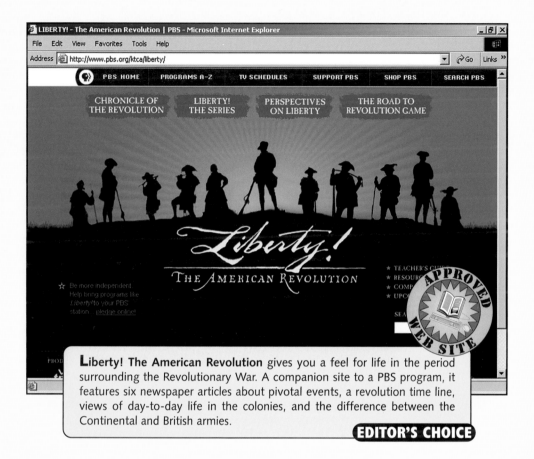

LIBERTY! - The American Revolution | PBS - Microsoft Internet Explorer

File   Edit   View   Favorites   Tools   Help

Address http://www.pbs.org/ktca/liberty/   Go   Links

PBS HOME   PROGRAMS A-Z   TV SCHEDULES   SUPPORT PBS   SHOP PBS   SEARCH PBS

CHRONICLE OF THE REVOLUTION   LIBERTY! THE SERIES   PERSPECTIVES ON LIBERTY   THE ROAD TO REVOLUTION GAME

Liberty!

THE AMERICAN REVOLUTION

☆ Be more independent
Help bring programs like
Liberty! to your PBS
station... pledge online!

★ TEACHER'S GUIDE
★ RESOURCES
★ COMP
★ UPC

SEA

Liberty! The American Revolution gives you a feel for life in the period surrounding the Revolutionary War. A companion site to a PBS program, it features six newspaper articles about pivotal events, a revolution time line, views of day-to-day life in the colonies, and the difference between the Continental and British armies.

EDITOR'S CHOICE

fired in the Revolutionary War. By July of the next year, Americans were ready to shed their ties to Great Britain. They stated their intent to be free in the Declaration of Independence.

→ THE STATES WRITE THEIR OWN CONSTITUTIONS

The colonists had a task ahead of them. They needed to create their new states. They did this by writing constitutions. A constitution is a document that sets up how a government will work. It is also a kind of agreement that says the people agree to be represented by the government.[3] Most also chose to include a bill of rights as part of their constitution. They based their bill of rights on British laws. There was some irony in this approach. After all, they were fighting a war to be free of the British. Still, they looked to the loftiest of British laws when they formed their new governments. In the year 1215, the British had adopted the Magna Carta. Magna Carta means "great charter" in Latin. The Magna Carta said that the king had to respect the rights of the people. However, not all kings held up their end of the deal. Many years later, in 1689, the people of England tried again. They bargained with the Crown to draw up a law that would protect their freedoms. The result came to be known as the English Bill of Rights. Americans looked to these laws for ideas.

THE NEED FOR A FEDERAL GOVERNMENT

The thirteen states worked with one another to win the war. Once the war was over, they still needed to work together. They were in debt. They had borrowed money to fight the Revolution. Now they needed to pay it back. A central government would bind the states together, and could uphold the law. It could make sure the states all pitched in to help. But Americans did not want a strong central

Historical Documents: The Magna Carta

Signed in 1215, the Magna Carta influenced the Bill of Rights centuries later. This site provides the text, a summary, a description of its influence and legacy, and a photograph of the 1297 version, which is housed in the National Archives Rotunda alongside other important formative documents.

Access this Web site from http://www.myreportlinks.com

government. They did not want a distant leader telling them what to do. They wanted to rule themselves at a local level. Many Americans were wary of any kind of central government at all. Memories of British rule were fresh in their minds.

However, the delegates from the states realized they would need to work together. They signed a document called the Articles of Confederation, which only allowed them to form a very weak central government. The delegates made it that way on purpose. That way the federal government could never have too much power over the states. The American people soon saw it was much too weak to work. The central government did not have an army. How would it enforce laws? It could not raise money. How would it pay off the war debt? The states agreed to send a new group of delegates to Philadelphia. The delegates would fix the problems.

→ THE CONSTITUTIONAL CONVENTION OF 1787

In the summer of 1787, fifty-five men came to the city of Philadelphia. Each of the states, except for Rhode Island, sent men to speak for them. It was a sweltering hot summer that year. The delegates met for many weeks. They listened to one another

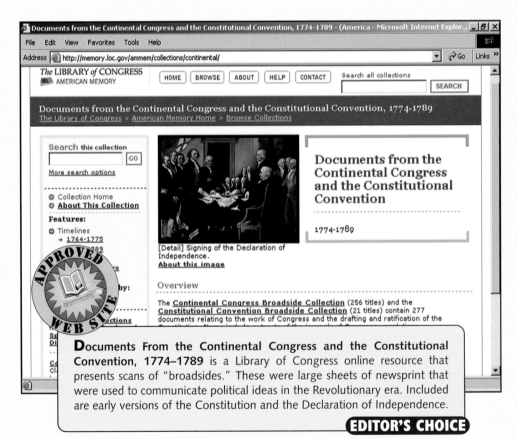

Documents From the Continental Congress and the Constitutional Convention, 1774–1789 is a Library of Congress online resource that presents scans of "broadsides." These were large sheets of newsprint that were used to communicate political ideas in the Revolutionary era. Included are early versions of the Constitution and the Declaration of Independence.

EDITOR'S CHOICE

and they hammered out the details. They strove to design a government that would be strong. They also wanted a government that the people could trust. They decided not to fix the Articles of Confederation. Instead, they abandoned the Articles of Confederation and started over. They wrote a brand new constitution. They set down on paper what powers the central government should have. They set up the structure of the government, too. Many of the men had experience with such matters because they had helped to write their state constitutions.

⊜ Government for the People

The delegates knew they had an important task to complete. If the new government was to work, the people would need to trust in it. They had to create a government that would represent the will of the people. To be sure of this, the founders did a wise thing. They split up the government into three different branches. The three branches share the power. They work together, and they also watch over one another. They make sure one branch does not grow too powerful.

What are the three branches? First there is the legislative branch. That is the U.S. Congress. The legislative branch writes the laws. The Congress is made up of two houses. These are the Senate and the House of Representatives. The second branch is the executive branch. That is the office of the president. The executive branch enforces the laws. The judicial branch is the third branch. This branch is the federal courts. The Supreme Court is the highest court in the United States. The judicial branch interprets the laws.

The Founding Fathers wrote the Constitution in an effort to establish a strong government. While doing so, they also set limits on how strong the federal government could be.

→GEORGE MASON: DEFENDER OF HUMAN RIGHTS

George Mason was one of the delegates at the Constitutional Convention. He spoke for his home state of Virginia. Mason was a planter, not a lawyer or a politician. But he was well known in his state. He had written Virginia's Bill of Rights. Mason did not like the new Constitution. He thought it took too much power away from the states. He spoke up for a bill of rights. He felt strongly that freedoms must be protected by a constitution. Others did not agree because they felt that the protections already written into the Constitution were sufficient. They did not include a bill of rights, and Mason was furious. He refused to sign the final draft of the Constitution. To his eyes, it did not do enough to protect basic human rights. He was sure no good would come of it.[4]

File   Edit   View   Favorites   Tools   Help

Address http://www.gunstonhall.org/

Gunston Hall Plantation

Home of George Mason

Visit
Events
George Mason
Mason Family
House & Grounds
Teacher Resources
Research Resources
Weddings & Rentals
Museum Shop

"That all men are born equally free and independent, and have certain inherent natural Rights . . . among which are the Enjoyment of Life and Liberty, with the Means of acquiring and possessing Property, and pursueing and obtaining Happiness and Safety."

-- George Mason. *Virginia Declaration of Rights*, May, 1776.

The words of George Mason (1725-1792) have inspired generations of Americans and others throughout the world. Mason was among the first to call for such basic American liberties
[More

Statesman and patriot George Mason is known as the "Father of the Bill of Rights." The **Gunston Hall Plantation** Web site describes his 550-acre home in Fairfax, Virginia. There is information for visitors, a time line of events related to the American Revolution and the development of the Bill of Rights, documents on human rights, and more.

→JAMES MADISON: FATHER OF THE CONSTITUTION

James Madison also came from Virginia. Madison did a great thing for history by keeping a daily journal. He wrote about what went on behind closed doors at the convention. Without his journal we would not know much about the making of the Constitution. At first, Madison did not like the idea of a bill of rights. He was not alone. Most of the delegates did not think a bill of rights was a good idea. They even thought a list of rights might do some harm. What about rights not on the list? Would the government be able to take them away?[5]

Later Madison changed his mind. In fact, it was he who eventually wrote the Bill of Rights. What made Madison change his mind? His friend and colleague Thomas Jefferson did. Jefferson was the author of the Declaration of Independence. Yet Jefferson did not take part in writing the Constitution. He was busy in Paris serving as ambassador to France. He and Madison wrote letters back and

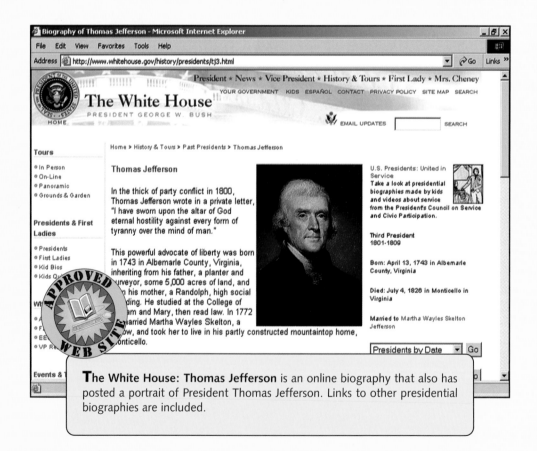

The White House: Thomas Jefferson is an online biography that also has posted a portrait of President Thomas Jefferson. Links to other presidential biographies are included.

forth. Madison wrote about how some people wanted to include a bill of rights, and Jefferson agreed with them. He felt it was the right thing to do. A bill of rights would protect the rights of citizens. It would keep the central government in line. It would help Americans gain trust in the new government.[6]

⊜ To Ratify or Not?

Thirty-nine delegates signed the final draft of the Constitution. Now it was up to the states. Nine of thirteen states had to accept, or ratify the Constitution. Delaware was the first state to act. Every last man who had a vote chose to accept it. There was no debate. It did not go so smoothly in other states. People split into two camps. One was the Federalists. They wanted to see the new Constitution pass. They felt that a strong federal government was a good idea. The Anti-Federalists did not agree. They did not like the new Constitution, and thought it needed a bill of rights and took too much power away from the states.

The Federalists knew the Constitution could work and had great faith in it. They were sure that most people would support the Constitution if they knew more about it. Somehow they had to spread the word. So, a small group published a series of essays called *The Federalist Papers*. At the time, no one knew exactly who wrote them. Today we do know. The authors were three of the founders—Alexander Hamilton, John Jay, and James Madison. The essays were widely read. They helped convince Americans that the Constitution was a good idea.

The Anti-Federalists did not want the states to ratify the Constitution. They wrote the "Address and Reasons of Dissent of the Minority of the Convention." It talked about the need for a bill of rights. It had some strong points. People listened. The public liked the idea of a bill of rights. Some

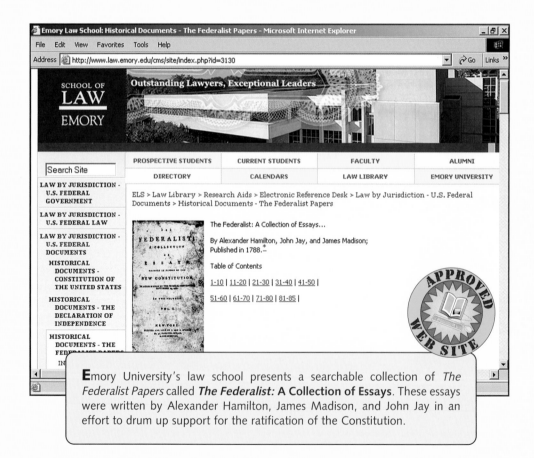

Emory University's law school presents a searchable collection of *The Federalist Papers* called ***The Federalist: A Collection of Essays***. These essays were written by Alexander Hamilton, James Madison, and John Jay in an effort to drum up support for the ratification of the Constitution.

states voted for the Constitution. They also made it clear they wanted to see a bill of rights added. They added lists of changes they would like.

In June 1788, New Hampshire took its vote. It voted in support of the Constitution. It was the ninth state to do so. Officially, the Constitution had passed. It only needed the vote from nine states to become law. There was just one problem. The state of Virginia had not agreed to it. Without the support of that state, it would never work. Virginia was a big state with many people. The debate among them was intense. While the nation looked on, Virginia took a vote. They voted to accept it. The Constitution had passed!

⊖Adding the Bill of Rights

The U.S. Congress met for the first time ever in 1789. President George Washington gave them a job to do. He asked that they resolve the debate about a bill of rights. Most of the members were Federalists. They were happy with the Constitution the way it was. They saw no need to add a bill of rights. James Madison took up the cause. He saw that a bill of rights was important to many citizens and knew more people would back the new federal Constitution if it had a bill of rights. He realized that if he wrote a bill of rights, he could control the outcome. It might be dangerous to leave a bill of rights to the Anti-Federalists. If

George Washington asked Congress to resolve the issue of whether the Constitution needed a Bill of Rights. James Madison, a fellow Virginian, took up the cause. Shown here are George Washington (top), Thomas Jefferson (bottom left), James Madison (bottom center), and John Adams (bottom right).

AMERICAN STAR.

THOMAS JEFFERSON.

JAMES MADISON.

OHN ADAMS.

they made a change to the Constitution, they might try to weaken it. Madison, and most of Congress, did not want that to happen. They had worked hard to write the Constitution and at securing its ratification.

Madison wrote a draft of a bill of rights. He looked to the states for ideas, and came up with a list of amendments. These amendments protected the rights of ordinary citizens. They also kept the powers of the states safe. Next he went about getting his fellow congressmen to agree. Most did not want to see any change to the Constitution—not so soon. Madison, though, worked hard. He succeeded in changing the minds of the Federalists in Congress. They sent a proposal to the states. If the states agreed, the Congress would amend the Constitution and add a bill of rights.

The Bill of Rights that Congress sent to the states had twelve amendments, not ten.

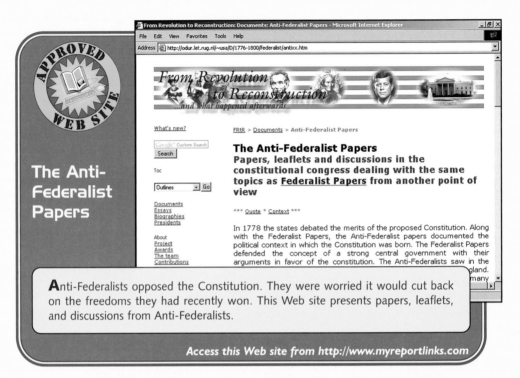

Anti-Federalists opposed the Constitution. They were worried it would cut back on the freedoms they had recently won. This Web site presents papers, leaflets, and discussions from Anti-Federalists.

Access this Web site from http://www.myreportlinks.com

The states did not agree to all twelve. The first two on the list did not make the final cut. One of the discarded amendments put a limit on the number of representatives in Congress. The other stated that Congress could not give itself a pay raise in the middle of a term. This one eventually became the Twenty-seventh Amendment in 1992. The Bill of Rights took effect in December 1791. The Anti-Federalists heaved a collective sigh of relief. At last, their rights were secured. Well, most of them felt relieved. George Mason was still not at ease. He was unhappy with the Constitution, right up to the day he died.[7]

UNDERSTANDING THE BILL OF RIGHTS

Do you know what freedoms the Bill of Rights protects? According to polls, many Americans do not.[1] We take these rights for granted. But how can we stand up for our rights if we do not know what they are?

→ THE FIRST AMENDMENT: FREEDOM TO BE DIFFERENT

The government can never represent all of the people, all of the time. At best, it can represent most of the people. The candidates who get the most votes win the elections. But what about the people who do not agree with them? That is where the First Amendment comes in. It protects those who think in a different way. In America, everyone has the right to his or her own ideas, even when most people do not agree with them. At the time the Bill of Rights was written, Americans had just fought a war for their freedom. They knew what it was like not to agree with the government. They knew what it was like to be afraid to practice their own religions. They wanted their new country to be different. They

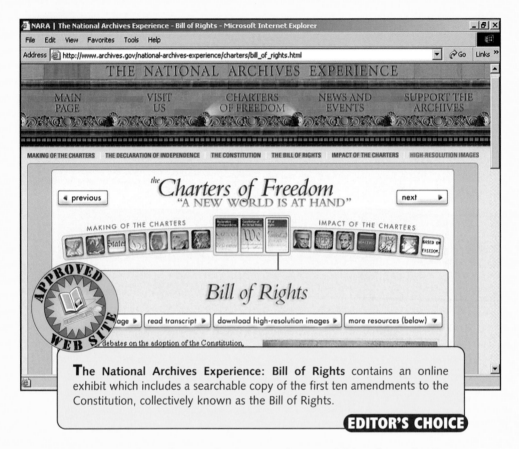

The National Archives Experience: Bill of Rights contains an online exhibit which includes a searchable copy of the first ten amendments to the Constitution, collectively known as the Bill of Rights.

EDITOR'S CHOICE

wanted a place where people would be free, both now and in the future. The First Amendment was meant to keep America free. Many believe that the First Amendment is the most important one of all.[2] It protects freedom of speech, freedom of religion, and freedom of the press. It also protects the right to assemble and petition the government.

→FREEDOM OF RELIGION

If you are an American, you are free to follow any religion you choose to worship. In fact, you do not have to practice any religion at all. This is one of the rights guaranteed by the First Amendment. Also, the federal government may not create an official national religion. Many of the colonists had to flee the Old World. They left their homes in Europe to come to America. They felt they had no choice. In the Old World, they could not freely practice their religions. Yet some of the colonists did not learn. They made the exact same mistake that the British had. Take the Puritans, for example. They did not like the way they were treated in England. They fled across the seas and began the Plymouth Colony. They continued the tradition of mixing church with the state.

A Puritan preacher named Roger Williams brought the idea of freedom of religion to America. He believed that people should be free to practice the religion of their choosing no matter what it was.[3] The Puritans kicked him out of the Massachusetts Bay Colony. They did not approve of his ideas. Williams went south to what is now Rhode Island. There he founded the city of Providence. The First Amendment is based on Williams's ideas. It reminds us that the government must be separate from all churches.

➔ FREEDOM OF SPEECH

The Founding Fathers wanted to create a country led by its people. They knew the United States would work only if people took part. People had to

Americans United for Separation of Church and State is an advocacy group that deals with church-state issues. Its Web site describes its controversial views, its campaigns, and related court cases. Resources include downloadable brochures and a copy of *Church & State* magazine.

be free to argue and debate. They had to be free to talk about their ideas. The First Amendment makes sure Americans cannot be punished for their ideas. Their ideas do not have to be popular or nice. It does not matter if no one agrees with those ideas. Every person still has a right to speak.

Americans are proud of their right to free speech. Still, not all speech is protected. There are times when speech can be dangerous. Justice Oliver Wendell Holmes helped to define this. He wrote that even the strongest protection of free speech "would not protect a man in falsely shouting fire in a theater and causing a panic."[4] Fighting words are not all right, either. Someone cannot try to start a fight by saying mean things in a face-to-face confrontation. The courts have also upheld laws that protect people from obscene speech. Obscene speech is crass and offensive to most people.

➔FREEDOM OF ASSEMBLY AND PETITION

The First Amendment says people have the right to assemble peacefully. To assemble means to meet together. An assembly can be just a few people. It could also be many people. The Founding Fathers thought that people had a duty to talk about their government. The British had not allowed the colonists to do this. Citizens also have the right to petition. Both are ways for people to communicate their ideas to their leaders. They are ways to bring about change.

➔FREEDOM OF THE PRESS

The First Amendment also protects the freedom of the press. In the early days of the United States, the press meant newspapers and pamphlets. Today, television and the Internet are also forms of the press. The press reports the news. If the press is not free to report the news, then the people will not know what the government is up to. If the government is to represent the people, then people must know what it is doing. Sometimes people call the press the fourth

Freedom of the press is one of the protections guaranteed to United States citizens in the First Amendment.

PRESS

branch of the government. The press performs a vital job. Government officials are less likely to do corrupt things if they know people will soon read about it. Like many freedoms, the freedom of the press is not without limits. The press must think about whether a story would risk the nation's security. Also, the press cannot publish deliberate lies that cause financial or personal damage to someone.

➡ THE SECOND AMENDMENT: THE RIGHT TO BEAR ARMS

The Second Amendment says each state has the right to keep a militia. A militia is a trained army. It is not the same as the U.S. Army. The U.S. Army does not control the militias; the states do. In some countries around the world, the army is in charge. It rules even though the people do not want it to. The people do not have the means to fight back. The Founding Fathers made sure that could not happen in the United States. Each state may keep and train a militia. Today, the Army National Guard is an example of a militia.

The Second Amendment also says Americans have the right to keep and bear arms. Many Americans own guns. Some are hunters. They hunt turkey, deer, and other animals for food. Others hunt for sport. Some people have guns to protect themselves in case of attack. Some farmers and ranchers use guns. They need them to protect

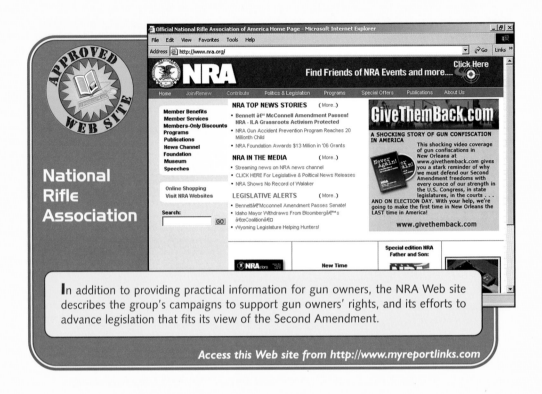

In addition to providing practical information for gun owners, the NRA Web site describes the group's campaigns to support gun owners' rights, and its efforts to advance legislation that fits its view of the Second Amendment.

Access this Web site from http://www.myreportlinks.com

their farm animals from wild animals. There is a downside, though. In 2002, more than thirty thousand people were killed by gunshot wounds.[5] Some people would like to make laws to help save lives. The laws would restrict how many guns are on the streets. Others argue that law-abiding citizens should not lose their right to own a gun. They believe the government should punish the criminal, not the weapon.

THE THIRD AMENDMENT: NO QUARTERING SOLDIERS

In colonial times, the British sent its army to America. The soldiers did not have a place to stay.

So, the British passed a new law. It was called the Quartering Act. It said that the colonists must feed and house the troops in their homes. The Americans did not like this one bit. How would you feel? What if armed soldiers took over your home? Americans thought it went against their rights. In fact, they even made mention of it in the Declaration of Independence. They never wanted to face that again. They made it against the law. The Third Amendment says the government cannot make you keep soldiers in your house in times of peace. It cannot in times of war, either, unless Congress passes a special law. This amendment does not mean much to Americans today because the United States government has never attempted to do something like the British had done.

THE FOURTH AMENDMENT: NO UNREASONABLE SEARCH AND SEIZURE

The Fourth Amendment protects people's right to a reasonable search and seizure if they are suspected of a crime. It implies a right to privacy by stating that the government may not search you or your home without probable cause. In most cases, the police need to obtain a warrant before a search can be done. A warrant is a document from a judge. A warrant must state what the police expect to find. It must say where they will search. The British had made the colonists pay a lot of

The Fourth Amendment grants United States' citizens the right to a reasonable search and seizure. If the police, however, have a reasonable suspicion that a person has been involved in a crime they have the right to search that person.

taxes. The colonists did not believe the taxes were fair. To avoid these taxes, some people turned to smuggling. The British tried to crack down on the smuggling. They searched people's homes, looking for illegal goods. British law said the police could not search without a warrant. However, the police got around this law. They had the judges issue warrants that were very broad. They allowed the police to search people anytime, for any reason. The colonists thought this kind of search was wrong. It was an abuse of power. It did not respect their right to privacy. The Founding Fathers wrote the Fourth Amendment to put a halt to this practice.

➔ THE FIFTH AMENDMENT: THE RIGHT TO DUE PROCESS

There are times when the government can take away a person's property. It may take away a person's freedom, but before that can happen, the person has the right to the due process of the law. The Fifth Amendment deals with people's rights in the court system. It protects people who are accused of a crime. It makes sure people get fair treatment, no matter who they are.

A capital crime is one that may lead to the death penalty. Anyone who is charged with a capital crime has the right to a grand jury. A grand jury is different from other juries. Most juries decide if someone is guilty or not. A grand jury

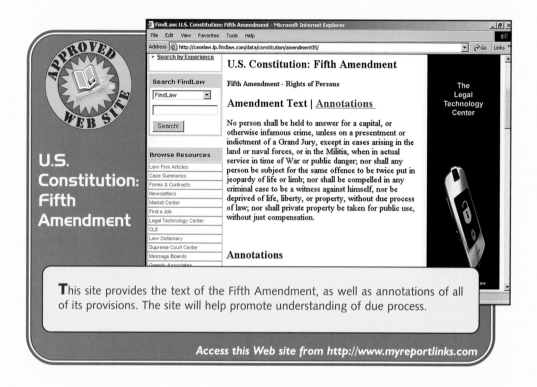

This site provides the text of the Fifth Amendment, as well as annotations of all of its provisions. The site will help promote understanding of due process.

Access this Web site from http://www.myreportlinks.com

does not. It looks at the facts of the case. It decides if there is enough information to bring the case to trial. The Fifth Amendment also says that once a person is found innocent, he or she is innocent. The person cannot face trial again for the exact same crime. If this were not so, the government could try a person over and over until the person was finally found guilty.

People do not have to answer questions during their trial. The Fifth Amendment says people have a right to not confess to crimes they are accused of. It is the government's job to prove the person is guilty. This is not true in some countries. In some places, people must prove they are innocent of the charges. In the United States, the jury must assume a person is innocent and then decide guilt based on the facts.

There are times when the government needs to take something a person owns for a public use. For instance, it might need more land to build a new road. When a government takes something away for the common good, it is called eminent domain. The owner is forced to give up property. It may be hard for the owner, but it is good for society as a whole. The Fifth Amendment says the government cannot just claim the property it needs. It must pay a fair price to the owner.

→THE SIXTH AND SEVENTH AMENDMENTS: THE RIGHT TO A JURY OF ONE'S PEERS

The Sixth Amendment does more to ensure the rights of people accused of crimes. It says that people have a right to a fair and speedy trial. People should not have to wait in jail for a long time before their trial. They must be judged innocent or guilty within a reasonable amount of time. They also have a right to a public trial. When a trial is open to the public, it will be more likely to be fair. The Sixth Amendment also says citizens have a right to counsel. That means the right to get the advice of a lawyer, and to be represented by a lawyer. Defendants also have the right to face the people who are accusing them of the crime. They

▲ *An image of an empty jury area. The Sixth Amendment guarantees the right to a speedy trial and for the verdict to be handed down by a jury.*

have a right to know what the charges are against them. That way they may prepare a defense.

The Seventh Amendment is also about juries. It says that people have a right to a jury trial in civil cases. In a civil case, no one goes to jail. Often a person who has been wronged sues someone else for money. Many civil cases never go to trial. A judge first looks over the case. The judge decides whether there is enough cause to pursue the case. The Seventh Amendment only applies to cases in federal courts.

➔THE EIGHTH AMENDMENT: NO EXCESSIVE BAILS OR FINES; NO CRUEL PUNISHMENT

The Eighth Amendment says that bails and fines cannot be excessive. Excessive means too much. They cannot be more than a person can possibly afford to pay. They also cannot be out of proportion with the crime. When police arrest a person for a serious crime, they soon take him or her to

This page presents images and the text of the English Bill of Rights (1689), discussing it in the context of citizenship in the United Kingdom. The Web page is called **Rise of Parliament: Making History.**

see a judge. The judge sets bail. If the suspect can pay the bail, he may go free until the trial. If he does not pay bail, he must wait in jail. The courts have ruled that judges do not always have to set bail. If they think the suspect may try to flee, they do not have to set bail. There is no

▲ *Any powers not given to the federal government in the language of the Constitution are automatically given to the states.*

bail if the suspect is dangerous. The courts do not keep the bail money. They hold it until the trial. If the suspect appears for trial, the bail is returned. Fines cannot be too high, either. A fine is a kind of punishment. Someone who is found to be guilty of a crime may have to pay a fine. Judges in England sometimes set fines so high that criminals could not hope to pay them. They were forced to stay in jail.

The Eighth Amendment also says that punishments must not be cruel or unusual. In colonial times, there were some very grisly ways of punishing people. Crowds threw stones at criminals until they died. Others were tied to a stake and burned alive. The Founding Fathers hoped to put an end to this type of torture. However, the Supreme Court has held that the death penalty does not violate the Eighth Amendment. For this reason, states are free to choose whether to use the death penalty.

new hampshire
vermont
maine
massachusetts
new york
rhode island
connecticut
pennsylvania
new jersey
ohio
delaware
west virginia
maryland
virginia
ky
north carolina
south carolina
georgia
florida

THE NINTH AMENDMENT: THE FREEDOM TO OTHER RIGHTS

The Ninth Amendment is very vague. It says that the government cannot take away any rights that the Constitution does not list. The people reserve these rights. But what are these mystery rights? Some of the Founding Fathers did not want a bill of rights. They thought it might limit the rights of the people. Anything that was not listed might be taken away by the government. The Ninth Amendment was put in so they need not worry. For hundreds of years, no one questioned this amendment. It was not until the twentieth century that the Supreme Court had a chance to rule on it.

THE TENTH AMENDMENT: POWERS HELD BY THE STATES

The Tenth Amendment speaks to the rights of the states. It says that the federal government gets all of its power from the Constitution. It can only be as strong as the Constitution makes it. Any other powers belong to the states. Like the Ninth Amendment, the Tenth Amendment is a bit vague. It does not define what other powers it is referring to. It was put in to reassure the states that they would not lose their rights.

DEFENDING FREEDOM— THE BILL OF RIGHTS AT WORK

4

*T*he Bill of Rights gives Americans great freedoms. Yet, in truth, it is only a piece of paper. In a perfect world, the government would always respect people's rights. In reality, people make mistakes. When that happens, Americans can go to the court system to seek to enforce their rights. Through the years, many cases have gone all the way to the U.S. Supreme Court. The Supreme Court has the final say. It decides whether a law is constitutional or not. The Supreme Court's decisions have further shaped and defined the Bill of Rights. Let us look at some of their decisions and see the Bill of Rights at work.

⮕SUBVERSIVE SPEECH: *SCHENCK V. UNITED STATES* (1919)

During World War I, Congress passed a law called the Espionage Act. The act made it against the law for an American to speak out against the war effort. The United States drafted men during World War I.

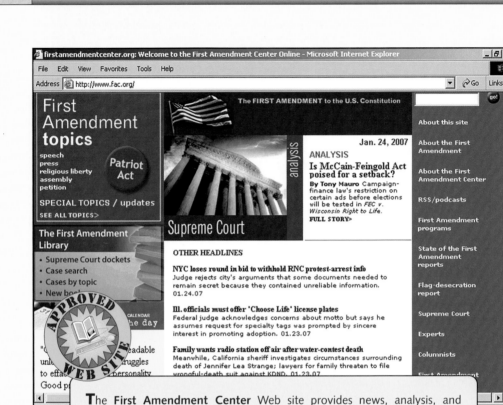

The FIRST AMENDMENT to the U.S. Constitution

First Amendment topics

speech
press
religious liberty
assembly
petition

Patriot Act

SPECIAL TOPICS / updates

SEE ALL TOPICS>

The First Amendment Library

• Supreme Court dockets
• Case search
• Cases by topic
• New books

Supreme Court

Jan. 24, 2007

ANALYSIS

Is McCain-Feingold Act poised for a setback?

By Tony Mauro Campaign-finance law's restriction on certain ads before elections will be tested in *FEC v. Wisconsin Right to Life.*

FULL STORY>

OTHER HEADLINES

NYC loses round in bid to withhold RNC protest-arrest info
Judge rejects city's arguments that some documents needed to remain secret because they contained unreliable information. 01.24.07

Ill. officials must offer 'Choose Life' license plates
Federal judge acknowledges concerns about motto but says he assumes request for specialty tags was prompted by sincere interest in promoting adoption. 01.23.07

Family wants radio station off air after water-contest death
Meanwhile, California sheriff investigates circumstances surrounding death of Jennifer Lea Strange; lawyers for family threaten to file wrongful-death suit against KDND. 01.23.07

About this site

About the First Amendment

About the First Amendment Center

RSS/podcasts

First Amendment programs

State of the First Amendment reports

Flag-desecration report

Supreme Court

Experts

Columnists

The First Amendment Center Web site provides news, analysis, and commentary on First Amendment issues, with sections on each First Amendment freedoms. Lesson plans are included for teachers.

A draft calls on men to serve as soldiers. Charles Schenck was opposed to the war, and so he decided to speak up for his beliefs. He sent pamphlets through the mail urging men to resist the draft. Police arrested Schenck for doing this. The Supreme Court ruled Schenk did not have a right to free speech in this case. They said his speech would be allowed in times of peace. Yet, in wartime, his pamphlets posed a "clear and present danger of inciting imminent, lawless action."[1] Congress repealed the Sedition Act, an amendment to the Espionage Act, in 1921.

➔ Fighting Words:
Chaplinsky v. New Hampshire (1942)

Walter Chaplinsky stood on a street while handing out pamphlets to people as they walked by. The pamphlets talked about his religion. Some of his words made passersby mad, so they stopped to argue. Eventually a riot broke out, and the police came to break it up. Chaplinsky swore at one of the policemen. He shouted at the officer and called him a "racketeer." The police arrested Chaplinsky. He had broken a state law against fighting words. Fighting words are very strong insults. They are said face-to-face for the purpose of starting a fight. They are not illegal because they are mean and hurtful. They are illegal because they pose a threat to the peace. Chaplinsky felt his words should be protected by the First Amendment. The Supreme Court disagreed. They ruled that the government may make laws against fighting words.[2]

➔ Hate Speech:
R.A.V. v. City of St. Paul (1992)

St. Paul, Minnesota had a city law against hate crimes. It defined hate crimes as those based on "race, color, creed, religion, or gender." Some teenagers broke this law by burning a cross on an African-American neighbor's lawn. In the past, racists have sometimes done this to intimidate African Americans. The police arrested the teenagers. The

The free speech rights of hate groups such as the Ku Klux Klan are protected by the Constitution. Although most people find their rhetoric disturbing and offensive, their ideas can be debated in an open forum.

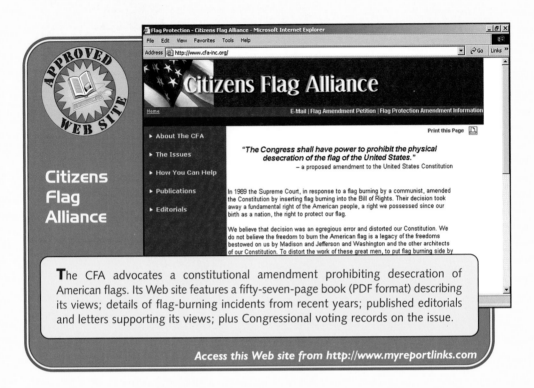

Flag Protection - Citizens Flag Alliance - Microsoft Internet Explorer

File   Edit   View   Favorites   Tools   Help

Address http://www.cfa-inc.org/

Citizens Flag Alliance

Home   E-Mail | Flag Amendment Petition | Flag Protection Amendment Information

Print this Page

▶ About The CFA

▶ The Issues

▶ How You Can Help

▶ Publications

▶ Editorials

"The Congress shall have power to prohibit the physical desecration of the flag of the United States."
– a proposed amendment to the United States Constitution

In 1989 the Supreme Court, in response to a flag burning by a communist, amended the Constitution by inserting flag burning into the Bill of Rights. Their decision took away a fundamental right of the American people, a right we possessed since our birth as a nation, the right to protect our flag.

We believe that decision was an egregious error and distorted our Constitution. We do not believe the freedom to burn the American flag is a legacy of the freedoms bestowed on us by Madison and Jefferson and Washington and the other architects of our Constitution. To distort the work of these great men, to put flag burning side by

Citizens Flag Alliance

The CFA advocates a constitutional amendment prohibiting desecration of American flags. Its Web site features a fifty-seven-page book (PDF format) describing its views; details of flag-burning incidents from recent years; published editorials and letters supporting its views; plus Congressional voting records on the issue.

Access this Web site from http://www.myreportlinks.com

teenagers were charged with committing a hate crime. A burning cross is a symbol of hate. In the American South, people burned crosses. They did it to scare African Americans and make them feel unwelcome. Clearly, what the teenagers did was wrong. But what about the law they had broken? Did it go against the First Amendment? The U.S. Supreme Court heard the case. The Court ruled that St. Paul was in the wrong. The hate crime law tried to limit what people could say. The law said people could not say hateful things about the color of someone's skin. But it did allow people to say hateful things about someone's political views. A law can not pick and choose what kinds of speech are allowed.[3]

Hate speech is protected under the First Amendment. The First Amendment protects the rights of all people to speak their mind—even if others would disagree with them. Oftentimes, it means protecting people who are saying some very ugly or mean things. What would happen if hate speech were not legal? There is a fine line between hate speech and other types of speech. Other kinds of speech that people do not like might be affected. Also, when people are not allowed to voice their ideas, those people become bitter. It is better to have hateful speech out in the open. That way people may honestly debate it.

➔ SYMBOLIC SPEECH: *TEXAS V. JOHNSON* (1989)

Freedom of speech covers more than just words. It means you are free to express yourself. The American flag is a symbol. It stands for the United States. A man named Gregory Lee Johnson got into big trouble when he set fire to an American flag. He did it as a form of protest. He did not like the policies of the government. He burned the flag outside the Republican National Convention in Dallas, Texas. The police came to arrest him. He had broken a Texas law that stated that people could not deface the American flag. Johnson took his case to the Supreme Court. He argued that he had a right to express his ideas under the First

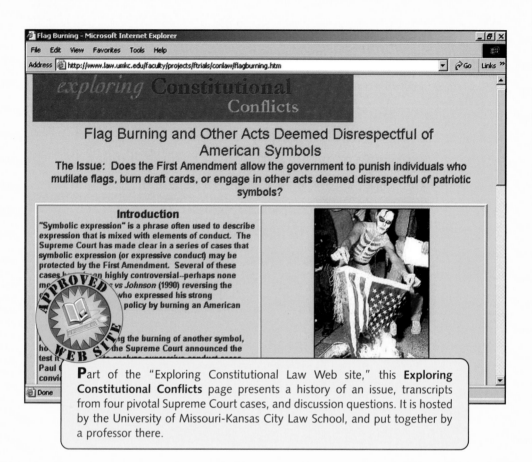

Flag Burning - Microsoft Internet Explorer

File   Edit   View   Favorites   Tools   Help

Address http://www.law.umkc.edu/faculty/projects/ftrials/conlaw/flagburning.htm   Go   Links »

exploring Constitutional
Conflicts

Flag Burning and Other Acts Deemed Disrespectful of American Symbols

The Issue: Does the First Amendment allow the government to punish individuals who mutilate flags, burn draft cards, or engage in other acts deemed disrespectful of patriotic symbols?

Introduction

"Symbolic expression" is a phrase often used to describe expression that is mixed with elements of conduct. The Supreme Court has made clear in a series of cases that symbolic expression (or expressive conduct) may be protected by the First Amendment. Several of these cases have been highly controversial--perhaps none more so than *Texas vs Johnson* (1990) reversing the conviction of a man who expressed his strong opposition to U.S. policy by burning an American flag.

...ng the burning of another symbol, however, the Supreme Court announced the test it uses in analyzing expressive conduct cases. Paul Cohen's conviction...

Part of the "Exploring Constitutional Law Web site," this **Exploring Constitutional Conflicts** page presents a history of an issue, transcripts from four pivotal Supreme Court cases, and discussion questions. It is hosted by the University of Missouri-Kansas City Law School, and put together by a professor there.

Amendment. In a 5 to 4 ruling, the Supreme Court agreed with him. They said burning a flag is a kind of speech. Free speech is the right of every American. Even when it is not popular, speech is still protected. Flag burning as a form of protest is protected by the First Amendment.[4]

The ruling was met with some anger and uproar. Many Americans felt it should be against the law to burn a flag. President George H. W. Bush was one of them. He asked for a constitutional amendment to protect the flag. There was not enough support in Congress for an amendment to pass. Congress did pass the federal Flag Protection Act. It made it against the law to burn a flag. The act was short-lived. The Supreme Court ruled the Act unconstitutional. Once again, the Court said flag burning fell under free speech. For the First Amendment to have meaning, it must protect all political debate, even debates regarding our most cherished symbols.[5] Congress may not pass a law to prohibit free speech. Flag burning remains a hot issue today. Some argue that respect for the flag is more important than freedom of speech. In June 2006, the House of Representatives passed a flag protection amendment proposal. It died on the Senate floor, where there was not enough support for the idea.

➡ FREEDOM OF ASSEMBLY:
EDWARDS V. SOUTH CAROLINA (1963)

A group of African-American students held a protest in 1961. They felt the state of South Carolina did not treat them fairly and segregated them because of the color of their skin. In an effort to change that, the students met on the grounds of the state capitol. The legislature was in session. Police came to arrest them. They charged the students with disturbing the peace. The state of South Carolina agreed with the police. The U.S. Supreme Court did not. It said the students were "exercising their basic constitutional rights."[6] The

A disagreement over an advertisement placed by Martin Luther King, Jr., led to the famous court case New York Times v. Sullivan. President Lyndon Johnson is seated in the background of this photo.

First Amendment says people have the right to assemble. It says people have the right to petition. They have the right to free speech. The students were simply using these rights to promote change. The Bill of Rights has helped Americans to make their country a better place. For instance, women did not have the right to vote until 1920. To get the vote, they signed petitions. They marched in the streets. They testified before Congress. They joined groups like the National Women's party. They could do these things thanks to the Bill of Rights.

LIBEL: *THE NEW YORK TIMES* V. *SULLIVAN* (1964)

The New York Times printed a full-page advertisement. The ad was about Dr. Martin Luther King, Jr. It talked about his fight for equal rights for African Americans in the South. The ad accused the police of bad conduct. L. B. Sullivan was the former commissioner of the Alabama police. He did not like that ad. He said the ad was libel. Libel is false words that ruin a person's good reputation. He sued *The New York Times*. A court in Alabama agreed with Sullivan. The ad did have some facts wrong. It did not make the police look very good. The court made *The New York Times* pay Sullivan half a million dollars in damages. *The New York Times* took the case to the Supreme Court. Sullivan's name did not appear in the ad. It was true, some

Formal prayer in public schools has been deemed a violation of the separation between church and state. Students in public schools, however, are allowed to pray on their own.

of the facts were wrong, and mistakes occasionally happen. However, many of the facts were right. If the police looked bad, it was their own fault. The Supreme Court reversed the Alabama court's decision. It said that a "robust debate on public issues is essential in a democracy."[7]

⊖ PRIOR RESTRAINT: *THE NEW YORK TIMES CO.* v. *UNITED STATES* (1971)

A worker at the Pentagon was angry about the Vietnam War. He leaked top secret papers to the press. He gave copies of the "Pentagon Papers" to two newspapers: *The New York Times* and *The Washington Post.* The Justice Department went to the court system to see what could be done. They wanted to stop the newspapers from printing the story. This is called prior restraint. To restrain means to stop or hold back. Prior means ahead of time. The government did not want the public to know about the top secret information. They argued that it would be a risk to the nation's security. For fifteen days, the courts banned the press from going public with the story. The United States government had never tried to stop the press through the courts before.[8] The Supreme Court knew it was an important case. They heard it right away. The Court lifted the ban, ruling that the Justice Department had not been able to prove that the story would risk the nation's security. The "top secret" information was several years old.

➔SCHOOL PRAYER: *ENGEL V. VITALE* (1962)

Students humbly sat at their desks with their heads bowed. Their teacher led them in saying the Lord's Prayer. Then the teacher asked a student to read from the Bible. In the 1960s, this was a common sight in public schools across America. For many students, this was in keeping with the Christian prayers they said at home. This was not true for all students, though. These prayers and readings made some parents uncomfortable because they went against their religious beliefs.

The state of New York tried to address this problem. The state made a law about prayers in school. The law mandated what kind of prayer the students could say. The prayer was very general, and it did not come from any specific religion. The Supreme Court struck down the law. It violated the First Amendment. The government cannot make laws about religion. It may not write prayers.[9] In other rulings, the Court went even further. It said that no prayers can be forced on a student as a part of public school. A student, though, could pray in school quietly to him or herself. The Court recognized that Americans are very religious people. They also recognized that freedom of religion is an important American value. Public schools must not promote religion.[10]

The official Web site of the **Brady Campaign to Prevent Gun Violence** describes the group's efforts to increase gun control. Also, discussed are the organization's involvement in political campaigns, legal issues, and action campaigns.

➔ THE RIGHT TO BEAR ARMS: *UNITED STATES V. MILLER* (1939)

In 1934, Congress passed the National Firearms Act. It restricted machine guns and sawed-off shotguns. These were not guns used by hunters. They were the weapons of choice for criminals. Not everyone thought it was a good idea. Some thought the act went against their Second Amendment rights. One case came before the Supreme Court. Police arrested Jack Miller and Frank Layton. The two men were carrying a sawed-off shotgun that was not registered. The National Firearms Act said that people had to register sawed-off shotguns. The men argued that the law went against the Second Amendment. A district court agreed with them. The Supreme Court, however, did not. The justices ruled that a sawed-off shotgun was not what the Founding Fathers meant to protect. Such a weapon is not used by militias.[11] The Court ruled that Congress can make some laws to control guns.

⊖ INTERPRETING THE SECOND AMENDMENT

Today, there is some heated debate over the right to bear arms. Some Americans feel that there is a need for gun control. They would like to see strict federal laws to keep guns out of the hands of criminals. Their opponents say these types of laws would not be constitutional. They point to the Second Amendment. They say it protects the right of the people to keep and bear arms without government involvement. People on both sides of the issue feel very strongly.

Does the Second Amendment really give people the right to keep and bear arms? Some people say no. They think it was meant to protect the state militias. They do not believe each citizen has a right to own a gun. That is because of the way the amendment reads. It says: "A well-regulated militia, being necessary to the security of a free state, the right of the people to keep and bear arms, shall not be infringed." The courts do not agree

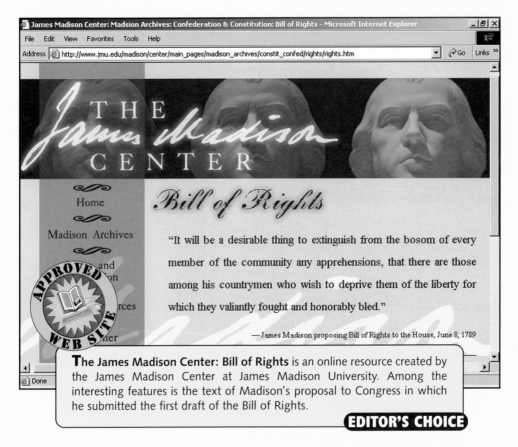

James Madison Center: Madsion Archives: Confederation & Constitution: Bill of Rights - Microsoft Internet Explorer

File   Edit   View   Favorites   Tools   Help

Address http://www.jmu.edu/madison/center/main_pages/madison_archives/constit_confed/rights/rights.htm

THE *James Madison* CENTER

Home

Madison Archives

Bill of Rights

"It will be a desirable thing to extinguish from the bosom of every member of the community any apprehensions, that there are those among his countrymen who wish to deprive them of the liberty for which they valiantly fought and honorably bled."

— James Madison proposing Bill of Rights to the House, June 8, 1789

The James Madison Center: Bill of Rights is an online resource created by the James Madison Center at James Madison University. Among the interesting features is the text of Madison's proposal to Congress in which he submitted the first draft of the Bill of Rights.

EDITOR'S CHOICE

with this way of reading the amendment. They have upheld the right of individuals to own guns. Yet they also have allowed some laws about guns.

➲THE FOURTEENTH AMENDMENT: RIGHTS FOR ALL

The Founding Fathers wrote the Bill of Rights to protect the people. Yet the Bill of Rights did not protect everyone at first. It did nothing for people brought to this country as slaves. The government did not treat them as people. It saw them as the property of the people who enslaved them. In

1865, the states ratified the Thirteenth Amendment making slavery against the law. Yet things did not change overnight. Some of the states still did not treat the freed people as citizens. More had to be done. Americans passed the Fourteenth Amendment. It said that anyone born in the United States is a citizen, and that even non-citizens should have equal protection. That means that they should be protected from unreasonable discrimination. In addition, they are entitled to due process of law (such as a hearing) before the government could take away their life, liberty, or property. The Bill of Rights protects each and every citizen.

James Madison foresaw that some state laws might threaten people's rights, just as much as the laws of the central government might. When he wrote the Bill of Rights, he tried to address this. He wrote one amendment that said the Bill of Rights would apply to the states, too. Congress did not choose to include it. For many years, state laws were not held to the same standard as federal laws. Finally, the Fourteenth Amendment addressed this problem. It says that the states may not deprive people of their rights, either. The Supreme Court has extended much of the Bill of Rights to the states.

5 THE SUPREME COURT UPHOLDS THE CONSTITUTION

Here are some more Supreme Court cases that show the Bill of Rights in action. As you read them, you may not always agree with what the Supreme Court rules. It may seem to you that the Court is hindering the hard work of the police. It may seem wrong to let a criminal go free. It might make you angry when the Court protects a person's right to say something hateful. The Bill of Rights is there for everybody. It does not choose between good people and bad people. It must protect the people who most need protection. Who needs to be protected the most? In some cases, they are people who are not very nice. We must be careful to stand up for the rights of all people. Only then can we be sure that the Bill of Rights will protect us, too. America is founded on the idea that it is better to let a guilty person go free than to punish an innocent person.

Police have arrested this man after a search turned up drugs on his person. The decision in the case Weeks v. United States made it clear that law enforcement officers must obtain warrants before they can search a person's home or office.

→ Search and Seizure: *Weeks v. United States* (1914)

The police entered a man's home without a warrant. They took some papers from his house. These papers showed the man had broken a law by selling lottery tickets through the mail. The police had proof the man was guilty. Yet they had gained that proof illegally. The Fourth Amendment says police need a warrant before they can search a person's home. The man, Mr. Weeks, took his case to the Supreme Court. The Supreme Court ruled that the police had to throw out the evidence, meaning they could not use it during a trial. Without the evidence, they could not convict the man of the crime. This is known as the Exclusionary Rule. This rule encourages police to follow the letter of the law. If the police conduct illegal searches, they cannot use the evidence during a trial.[1] In 1961, the Supreme Court said that states had to abide by the Exclusionary Rule as well.[2] The Court pointed to the Fourteenth Amendment. It says that the states must respect the rights of citizens, too.

→ Self Incrimination: *Miranda v. Arizona*

Long ago, in the days of ancient Rome, torture was used as a tool of investigation.[3] If police thought a person might be a criminal, they would ask him to confess. If he claimed to be innocent,

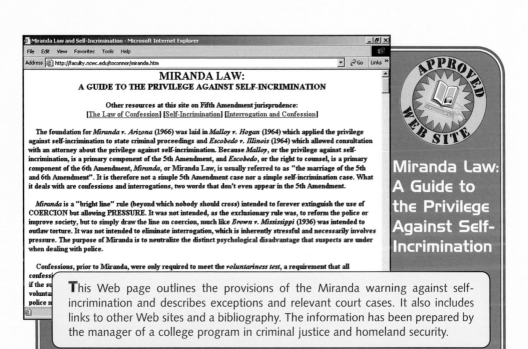

MIRANDA LAW:
A GUIDE TO THE PRIVILEGE AGAINST SELF-INCRIMINATION

Other resources at this site on Fifth Amendment jurisprudence:
[The Law of Confession] [Self-Incrimination] [Interrogation and Confession]

The foundation for *Miranda v. Arizona* (1966) was laid in *Malloy v. Hogan* (1964) which applied the privilege against self-incrimination to state criminal proceedings and *Escobedo v. Illinois* (1964) which allowed consultation with an attorney about the privilege against self-incrimination. Because *Malloy*, or the privilege against self-incrimination, is a primary component of the 5th Amendment, and *Escobedo*, or the right to counsel, is a primary component of the 6th Amendment, *Miranda*, or Miranda Law, is usually referred to as "the marriage of the 5th and 6th Amendment". It is therefore not a simple 5th Amendment case nor a simple self-incrimination case. What it deals with are confessions and interrogations, two words that don't even appear in the 5th Amendment.

Miranda is a "bright line" rule (beyond which nobody should cross) intended to forever extinguish the use of COERCION but allowing PRESSURE. It was not intended, as the exclusionary rule was, to reform the police or improve society, but to simply draw the line on coercion, much like *Brown v. Mississippi* (1936) was intended to outlaw torture. It was not intended to eliminate interrogation, which is inherently stressful and necessarily involves pressure. The purpose of *Miranda* is to neutralize the distinct psychological disadvantage that suspects are under when dealing with police.

Confessions, prior to *Miranda*, were only required to meet the *voluntariness test*, a requirement that all confess...

Miranda Law: A Guide to the Privilege Against Self-Incrimination

This Web page outlines the provisions of the Miranda warning against self-incrimination and describes exceptions and relevant court cases. It also includes links to other Web sites and a bibliography. The information has been prepared by the manager of a college program in criminal justice and homeland security.

Access this Web site from http://www.myreportlinks.com

they would torture him. They kept up the torture until he broke down and confessed. Torture is still used around the world even today. There is just one problem. Let us say you were faced with a choice: torture or confess. What would you do? It is easy to see how someone might choose to confess, even if she did not commit a crime or do anything wrong. A confession makes it easy for a court to decide if a person is guilty. But what if the only evidence the police have is a confession? We call that self-incrimination.

The Fifth Amendment says people have the right not to bear witness against themselves. A person may choose to remain silent. The person does not have to remain silent. He or she has a choice. But what if a person did not know about that right? This was the case with a man named Ernesto Miranda. The Arizona police thought he may have committed a serious crime. They arrested him and took him down to the police station. They asked him questions for several hours. After some time, Miranda confessed to the crime. Because he confessed, the court found him guilty. Miranda did not know he did not have to speak to the police. He did not know that whatever he did say would be used against him in court. He was not told that he had the right to the advice of a lawyer. The Supreme Court heard the case. They ruled that Miranda's Fifth Amendment rights had been violated. Miranda went free until his retrial. To make sure this did not happen again, the Court said that police must tell suspects about their rights.[4] Police now read suspects their "Miranda" rights. It has become a routine part of police work.

EMINENT DOMAIN: *LUCAS V. SOUTH CAROLINA COASTAL COUNCIL* (1992)

David Lucas bought two parcels of land. The land was beachfront property on a barrier island. The land cost a lot of money. Lucas

In some cases, local, state, and federal government can take land for public improvements through eminent domain. Under this rule the government must give the landowners just compensation for their property. Parts of the New Jersey Turnpike (a superhighway shown here during construction in 1951) were built on land that was taken through eminent domain.

had plans to build houses on the land. But two years after he bought it, South Carolina passed a new law. The law protected coastal areas. Now Lucas could no longer get a permit to build on his land. He took the state to court and argued that the land no longer had any value, thanks to the new law. By passing the law the state had effectively taken his land away from him. He could no longer use it in the way he wanted to. He pointed to the part of the Fifth Amendment which says that the government may not take away property without just compensation. The court awarded Lucas 1.2 million dollars.

The South Carolina Supreme Court reversed the lower court's decision. It held that South Carolina had every right to make the law. The state had not taken Lucas's land away from him. He still owned the land. They ruled that the state did not have to pay him anything. Lucas took his case to the U.S. Supreme Court. The Justices sent the case back to South Carolina. They said the state had a weak case. It would need to do more to prove that Lucas's intent to build went against public interest. If the state could not do this, they would have to compensate Lucas for his land.[5]

➡ Right to a Speedy Trial: Doggett v. United States (1992)

The Sixth Amendment says that Americans have a right to a speedy trial. It is not fair to expect a

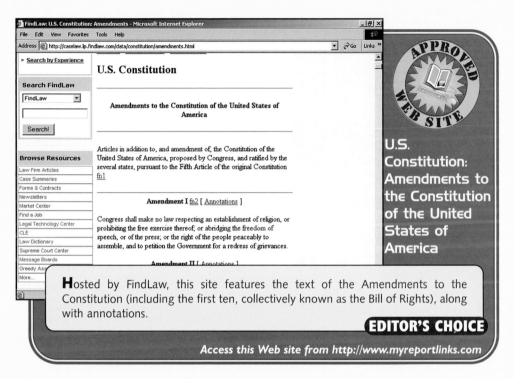

U.S.
Constitution:
Amendments to
the Constitution
of the United
States of
America

Hosted by FindLaw, this site features the text of the Amendments to the Constitution (including the first ten, collectively known as the Bill of Rights), along with annotations.

EDITOR'S CHOICE

Access this Web site from http://www.myreportlinks.com

person to wait a long time for his case to be heard. After all, as time passes, people forget things. It is too hard for a person to defend himself against charges from long ago. But, just how long is too long? The Sixth Amendment does not say. In 1992, the Supreme Court said eight and a half years was too long.[6] The case was *Doggett* v. *United States.*

In 1980, the police had evidence that a young man named Doggett was a drug dealer. But before they could arrest him, Doggett left the country. He was out of the country for two years. Agents at the Drug Enforcement Agency kept track of him for a while, but at some point they lost track of him. They were unaware that Doggett came back to the United States in 1982. He went to college and got married. He led a normal life and obeyed the law. The police eventually caught up to him. He was located in a routine check for outstanding warrants. The police arrested him on the old drug charges, even though it had been eight years ago. Doggett had not known about the charges. He argued that the case should be dropped. He pointed out his right to a speedy trial. The Supreme Court agreed.

RIGHT TO AN ATTORNEY: *GIDEON* V. *WAINWRIGHT* (1963)

The Sixth Amendment says that people accused of a serious crime have the right to counsel. Most people are not law experts. The law and all its rules can be very confusing. People need the help of a lawyer to argue their cases in court. What about people who cannot afford a lawyer? Take the case of Clarence Gideon. He was accused of breaking into a Florida pool hall. Gideon was poor. He did not have money to pay a lawyer. He asked the state to appoint a lawyer for him. The state refused. Gideon tried to defend himself during the trial. The jury found him guilty. The judge sentenced him to five years in prison. Gideon felt strongly that his trial had not been fair. He sat in his jail cell and hand wrote a petition to the Supreme Court.

The Supreme Court decided that the right to a fair trial is a "fundamental right." Like the right to free speech, the right to a fair trial is essential. Can a trial be fair if a person does not have the advice of a lawyer? The Court ruled that, no, it could not possibly be.[7] The states must protect people's right to a fair trial. The state had to appoint a defense lawyer at the state's expense under the Sixth and Fourteenth Amendments.

→ RIGHT TO A JURY TRIAL IN A CIVIL TRIAL

The Seventh Amendment gives the right to a jury trial in all civil cases more than twenty dollars. It seems like a funny amount today. Who would go to court over less than twenty dollars? Of course, twenty dollars used to be worth much more back then. The states do not have to abide by this right. It only applies to cases held in federal courts. So far, the Supreme Court has not extended it to the states under the Fourteenth Amendment.

→ THE DEATH PENALTY: CRUEL AND UNUSUAL PUNISHMENT?

The Eighth Amendment bans cruel and unusual punishment. What exactly does that mean? It means something different to us today than it did to the Founding Fathers. In their time, it was common to put a criminal to death in a public

Gallows such as those shown here were used in the past to execute people by hanging the criminals. Hangings are no longer practiced in the United States. The Eighth Amendment guarantees that a person will not suffer cruel or unusual punishment.

square. A crowd of people would come to watch. Today, that would not be acceptable. Times have changed, and so have people's ideas about what is cruel.

In 2005, sixty people were put to death in the United States.[8] Today, there is only one crime for which the sentence may be death. That is murder. Even so, some people do not agree with the death penalty. They do not think the government has the right to take away a person's life. They feel this punishment is cruel and unusual. Twelve states do not allow the death penalty at all. On the other hand, California, Texas, and Florida each have hundreds of criminals sitting on death row.

➡ FAIRNESS AND CAPITAL PUNISHMENT LAWS

In the 1970s, new data came out about the death penalty. The facts were disturbing. Poor people were much more likely to get the death penalty than wealthier people. Black people were more apt to be put to death than white people. The Supreme Court said that the death penalty was much too arbitrary. In *Furman* v. *Georgia* (1972), the Court ruled that the states' current death penalty laws violated the Eighth Amendment.[9] The Court found that the death penalty was not being applied in a fair way.

The states tried to make their court decisions fairer. They gave juries more guidance about when

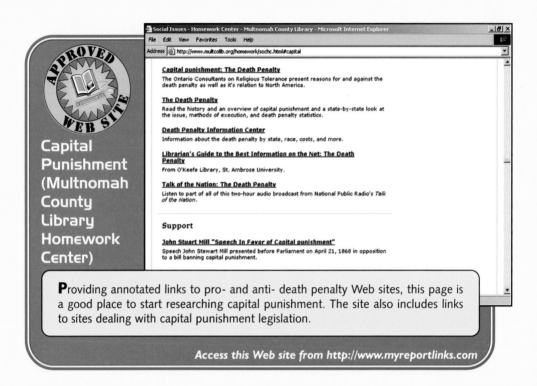

Capital
Punishment
(Multnomah
County
Library
Homework
Center)

Providing annotated links to pro- and anti- death penalty Web sites, this page is a good place to start researching capital punishment. The site also includes links to sites dealing with capital punishment legislation.

Access this Web site from http://www.myreportlinks.com

to use the death penalty. In 1976, the Supreme Court revisited the subject of the death penalty. It ruled that the states had done their best to fix their laws, and so the Court upheld those laws. Two justices did not agree. Justices Brennan and Marshall argued that any form of the death penalty was cruel. In 1988, the Supreme Court heard the case of *Thompson* v. *Oklahoma*. It ruled that a youth could not be sentenced to die.[10] The boy was fifteen when he took part in a murder. A year later, the Court set a limit on its protection of minors. It ruled that sixteen-year-olds were old enough to be tried as adults. They could legally get the death penalty. In 2005, the case *Roper* v. *Simmons* reversed that decision. It said a sixteen-year-old could not be executed for a capital crime.

➡ PRIVACY: *GRISWOLD* V. *CONNECTICUT* (1965)

Estelle Griswold was a counselor. Her job was to advise married couples. If a couple was not ready to have children, she told them about the option of birth control. Birth control is a way for couples to plan when they will have children. Birth control was against the law in Connecticut. The police charged her with breaking the law. She took her case to the Supreme Court. She argued that married couples had a right to privacy. The Court agreed. It said that birth control was a private matter. It was no business of the government.[11] Nowhere in the Bill of Rights does it say that people have a right to privacy. However, the First, Third, Fourth, Fifth and Fourteenth Amendments protect notions of privacy.

➡ RIGHT TO BE LET ALONE: *LOVING* V. *VIRGINIA* (1967)

The Fourteenth Amendment went a long way to ensure equal rights for all. The laws did not reflect this fairness for some time to come. In the 1960s, the state of Virginia had a law on the books saying it was against the law for people from different races to marry. Virginia was not alone. Many other

The mission of **Human Rights Watch** is "defending human rights worldwide." Its Web site presents information on its campaigns sorted geographically and by issue of their publications.

EDITOR'S CHOICE

states had similar laws. One couple, Richard Loving (a white man) and Mildred Jeter (a black woman) decided to challenge this law. The Supreme Court said this law was not right. It went against the Fourteenth Amendment. People should have the freedom to choose whom they will marry, regardless of the person's skin color.[12] The government has no right to interfere. Marriage is a private matter.

LIVING IN AMERICA: RECENT DEBATE ABOUT THE BILL OF RIGHTS

6

The Founding Fathers would be amazed by the world we live in. In their day, most newspapers came out just once a week. If you wanted to get a message to someone far away, you wrote a letter. There was no such thing as a telephone. Today's world moves much faster. The Internet has brought about a lot of changes. Anyone can look up information with the touch of a button. All it takes is a computer and access to the Internet. Anyone can put his or her ideas out there for others to see. The Internet is an amazing tool. It creates a true marketplace of ideas. Yet there is information online that is not meant for everyone to see. Some of it is indecent or obscene. Does the government have the duty to make sure the Internet is safe for children? How does freedom of speech work on the Internet? The United States is still sorting this out.

The **American Civil Liberties Union** Web site features information about its campaigns to assure that United States citizens are afforded their rights, including those established in the Bill of Rights.

➔FREE SPEECH AND THE INTERNET: *RENO* V. *AMERICAN CIVIL LIBERTIES UNION* (1997)

Do you have the right to listen to the radio without hearing swear words? Most Americans feel that they do. Congress has made laws to control the airwaves. The laws protect Americans from profane, indecent, and obscene material. There are laws about what can be shown on television, too. Most of all, these laws are in place to protect children. For instance, there are laws that say movie theaters may not show R-rated movies to kids. The Internet is a different story. It is not so easy to restrict. Kids can log on at home, at school, or at a library.

Congress would like to make the Internet safe for kids to use. There is just one problem. How can it be safe for children and still respect the right to free speech? Congress has tried to tackle this problem. It passed the Communications Decency Act in 1996. The act protected kids under the age of eighteen. It made it against the law to send indecent material over the Internet to them. The Supreme Court struck down parts of this act in *Reno* v. *ACLU*. The American Civil Liberties Union (ACLU) is a group that defends the Bill of Rights.

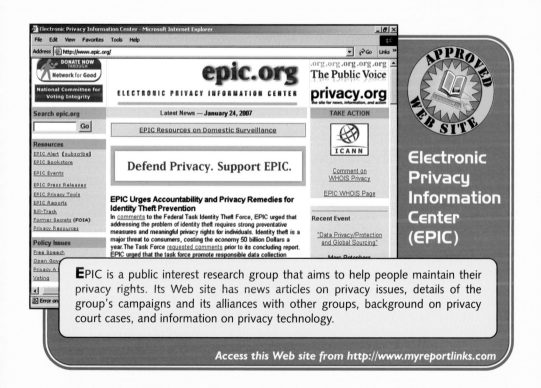

EPIC is a public interest research group that aims to help people maintain their privacy rights. Its Web site has news articles on privacy issues, details of the group's campaigns and its alliances with other groups, background on privacy court cases, and information on privacy technology.

Access this Web site from http://www.myreportlinks.com

It challenged the act. It believed it went too far. A district court agreed with the ACLU. Janet Reno was the U.S. Attorney General under President Bill Clinton. She took the case to the Supreme Court. The Supreme Court upheld the lower court's decision. The Court ruled that parts of the act were far too broad. The act went so far that it put limits on good information that adults might find useful, even if it was inappropriate for young people. Justice Stevens wrote that it would limit such educational material as "artistic images that include nude subjects, and arguably that card catalog of the Carnegie Library."[1] It went against people's right to free speech. Plus, the Court said people who want to protect children do have some options. They can put filters on their computers.[2] A filter is a kind of software. It limits what the person who is using the computer can access.

United States v. American Library Association (2003)

In 2000, Congress tried again. It passed the Children's Internet Protection Act. It forced libraries to put filters on their computers. If the libraries did not have filters, they did not get federal money. Some libraries and their patrons did not like this. They argued that the filters were too broad. They were not sensitive enough. They blocked out too much. The Supreme Court disagreed. It upheld the Children's Internet Protection Act in 2003, saying that a librarian could turn off the filters if a patron requested it for a legitimate purpose such as research.

⮕ RIGHTS OF STUDENTS AT PUBLIC SCHOOL

Does the Bill of Rights protect students while they are at a public school? The Supreme Court has considered this question many times. The answer is a resounding yes! Students do not give up all their rights when they step into the schoolroom. Yet, the school also has a duty. The principal and teachers need to keep school a safe place for learning. It can be a tough balancing act. Read on to see what rights the Supreme Court has upheld for students.

⮕ *TINKER V. DES MOINES INDEPENDENT COMMUNITY SCHOOL DISTRICT* (1969)

John and Mary Beth Tinker and their friend Christopher Eckhardt were students in 1965. They attended public school in Des Moines, Iowa. They did not think the United States should be at war in Vietnam. They wore black armbands to school in protest. In doing so, they broke a school rule. The rule said students could not take part in protests at school. The school feared that protests would disrupt classes. The school punished the students by suspending them from school. The students did

Mary Beth Tinker (shown here) was one of the defendants in the case Tinker v. Des Moines.

not think the school rule was fair. They thought it violated their right to free speech. They took their fight all the way to the Supreme Court. It reversed the lower courts' rulings. In a vote of 7 to 2, the justices stood up for the students' right to freedom of speech. Justice Abe Fortas wrote the majority opinion. He stated: "First Amendment rights . . . are available to teachers and students. It can hardly be argued that either students or teachers shed their constitutional rights to freedom of speech or expression at the schoolhouse gate. . ."[3] He went on to say that because teachers are shaping American citizens, students need to learn about their rights. They need to learn that these rights are respected. They are not just words on paper that can be ignored when they are inconvenient.[4] Fortas felt that wearing an armband is a silent form of protest. It does not disrupt school.

→*HAZELWOOD SCHOOL DISTRICT V. KUHLMEIER* (1988)

The Supreme Court said students have a right to free speech in the case of Tinker v. Des Moines. What about other First Amendment rights? Do students have those as well? In the 1980s, the Court heard another landmark case. It was about freedom of the press in public schools. In the city of St. Louis, Missouri, students could take a class in journalism. As part of their class, they published the

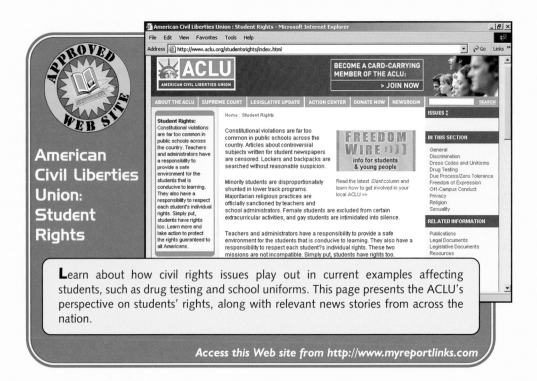

American
Civil Liberties
Union:
Student
Rights

Learn about how civil rights issues play out in current examples affecting students, such as drug testing and school uniforms. This page presents the ACLU's perspective on students' rights, along with relevant news stories from across the nation.

Access this Web site from http://www.myreportlinks.com

school newspaper. They had the help and advice of their teacher. One year, the students worked extra hard on the paper, and wrote about some sensitive topics. They wrote about teenagers who were pregnant and the hardships they faced. They wrote about divorce and how hard it can be on kids.

Finally, the paper was ready to go to the press for printing. First, the school principal read over the proofs. He did not think some of the stories were appropriate for younger students at the school. He decided not to print the stories. The students were not told that their stories had been censored. They only found out when they got the newspapers back from the printers. They were mad and disappointed. They felt the principal had not respected their First Amendment rights. They took their case to court. The Supreme Court, in a 5 to 3 vote, supported the principal's actions. It ruled that principals have the right to censor their students' articles. A school newspaper is the voice of the school. It should not disrupt the education of the students. The school can have some rules about what it will print. It would have been wrong if the principal punished the students for writing the articles.[5] But that did not happen. He simply did not print the articles.

➡ *NEW JERSEY V. T.L.O.* (1985)

Does a school need a warrant to search a student? The Supreme Court had a chance to rule on this in 1985. School officials thought a student might have illegal drugs. They searched her belongings and found marijuana. The student argued that the search went against her Fourth Amendment rights. The school did not have a warrant. The student had to go in front of a juvenile delinquent court. Should the evidence be thrown out, since the searchers did not have a warrant? The student argued that yes, it should. The New Jersey Supreme Court agreed.

The U.S. Supreme Court reversed the ruling. Justice White wrote the majority opinion. He admitted that students do have a right to privacy.

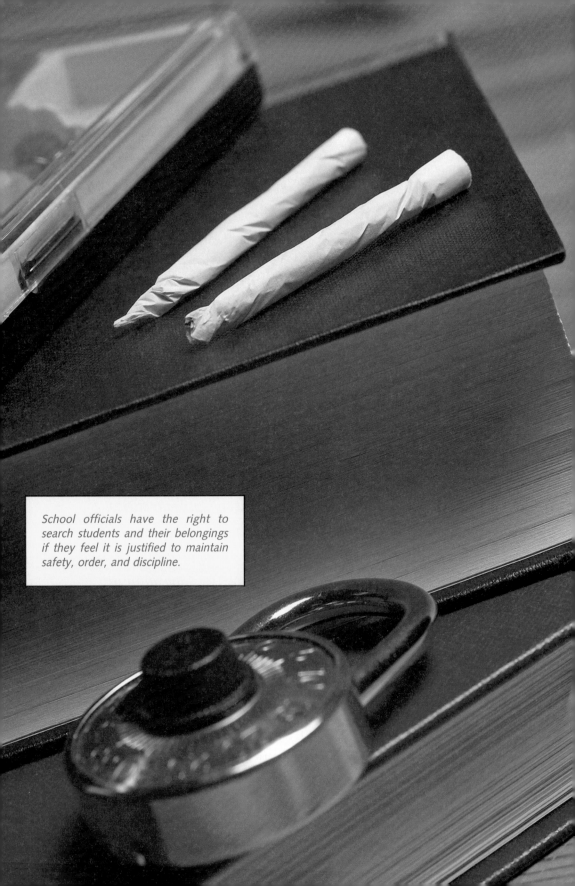

School officials have the right to search students and their belongings if they feel it is justified to maintain safety, order, and discipline.

Parents can search their children at any time. School officials do not have the same right to search as parents do. Justice White also wrote that public schools must be kept safe. Students at public schools need to be kept safe as well. That is part of the school officials' jobs. To maintain safety, order, and discipline, sometimes school officials can search a student. First, they must have a good reason to conduct a search.[6]

VERNONIA SCHOOL DISTRICT 47J V. ACTON (1995)

Is it reasonable for a school to require random drug testing of students? In 1995, the Supreme Court ruled on this issue. An Oregon school had a policy about drug testing. Students who joined a sports team were subjected to random tests for drugs in their urine. One student refused to do it, so he was not allowed to join the team. He and his parents felt the tests infringed upon his right to privacy. The school said that it had a good reason for the drug tests. Students on drugs were more likely to be hurt while playing sports.

The case went all the way to the Supreme Court. The Court upheld the school's right to test students for drugs. The school had a right to make sure athletes were not on drugs. Students did not have to join an athletic team. They had a choice.

If they chose to be part of the team, then they gave up the right to privacy in regards to drug testing.[7]

→ PRAYER IN PUBLIC SCHOOL: *LEE V. WEISMAN* (1992)

Can students and teachers say prayers as part of their day at public school? In the 1960s, the Supreme Court ruled no, not as a part of the official school day. Many Americans did not agree. As a result, some prayers still went on in public schools. In 1992, the Supreme Court ruled again on prayer in schools. They heard the case of Daniel Weisman. His daughter was a student at a middle school. When it came time for her class to

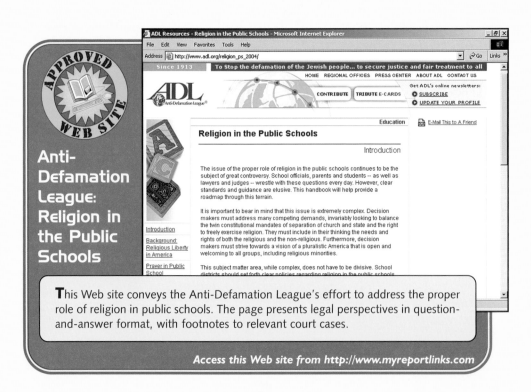

Anti-Defamation League: Religion in the Public Schools

This Web site conveys the Anti-Defamation League's effort to address the proper role of religion in public schools. The page presents legal perspectives in question-and-answer format, with footnotes to relevant court cases.

Access this Web site from http://www.myreportlinks.com

graduate, the school held a ceremony. The principal invited a Jewish rabbi to speak. The rabbi led the students in two short prayers. Mr. Weisman argued that the government—in this case, the school—could not force students to take part in prayers. The school board backed up the actions of the principal. Any student who did not like the prayer could simply remain silent. George H. W. Bush was the president of the United States at the time. He agreed with the school board. He asked the Supreme Court to allow prayer at school ceremonies. However, the Supreme Court did not agree with the president. It sided with the student. Justice Kennedy wrote: "A reasonable dissenter of high school age could believe that standing or remaining silent signified her own participation in . . . the exercise."[8] The First Amendment says the government may not endorse religion. It may not sponsor prayers. In 2000, the Court upheld this idea yet again. It ruled that students could not lead a prayer over a loudspeaker before a football game.

⇒Learn Your Rights, Voice Your Opinions

As you can see, the Bill of Rights is always at work. The Supreme Court makes decisions every year that affect the rights of Americans. Will the United States always be the land of the free? History shows us that governments rise and fall. There is only

The Bill of Rights and the First Amendment guarantee freedom of expression to every individual in the United States. Voice your ideas and speak up for what you believe in.

one way for America to continue as a democracy. The people of America have to make it happen. We must value our Bill of Rights. We must make sure that the government values it, too. You can do this by learning about your rights as an American. You can voice your ideas. You can use your rights to speak up for what you believe in. You can change the world into a better place. After all, the U.S. Constitution is a document that has proved to be adaptable to the changing times.

The Constitution of the United States

The text of the Constitution is presented here. All words are given their modern spelling and capitalization. Brackets [ ] indicate parts that have been changed or set aside by amendments.

Preamble

We the People of the United States, in Order to form a more perfect Union, establish Justice, insure domestic Tranquillity, provide for the common defence, promote the general Welfare, and secure the Blessings of Liberty to ourselves and our Posterity, do ordain and establish this Constitution for the United States of America.

Article I
The Legislative Branch

Section 1. All legislative powers herein granted shall be vested in a Congress of the United States, which shall consist of a Senate and House of Representatives.

The House of Representatives

Section 2. The House of Representatives shall be composed of members chosen every second year by the people of the several states, and the electors in each state shall have the qualifications requisite for electors of the most numerous branch of the state legislature.

No person shall be a Representative who shall not have attained to the age of twenty five years, and been seven years a citizen of the United States, and who shall not, when elected, be an inhabitant of that state in which he shall be chosen.

Representatives and direct taxes shall be apportioned among the several states which may be included within this union, according to their respective numbers, [which shall be determined by adding to the whole number of free persons, including those bound to service for a term of years, and excluding Indians not taxed, three fifth of all other persons]. The actual Enumeration shall be made within three years after the first meeting of the Congress of the United States, and within every subsequent term of ten years, in such manner as they shall by law direct. The number of Representatives shall not exceed one for every thirty thousand, but each state shall have at least one Representative; [and until such enumeration shall be made, the state of New Hampshire shall be entitled to chuse three, Massachusetts eight, Rhode Island and Providence Plantations one, Connecticut five, New York six, New Jersey four, Pennsylvania eight, Delaware one, Maryland six, Virginia ten, North Carolina five, South Carolina five, and Georgia three].

When vacancies happen in the Representation from any state, the executive authority thereof shall issue writs of election to fill such vacancies.

The House of Representatives shall choose their speaker and other officers; and shall have the sole power of impeachment.

The Senate

Section 3. The Senate of the United States shall be composed of two Senators from each state, [chosen by the legislature thereof,] for six years; and each Senator shall have one vote.

Immediately after they shall be assembled in consequence of the first election, they shall be divided as equally as may be into three classes. The seats of the Senators of the first class shall be vacated at the expiration of the second year, of the second class at the expiration of the fourth year, and the third class at the expiration of the sixth year, so that one third may be chosen every second year; [and if vacancies happen by resignation, or otherwise, during the recess of the legislature of any state, the executive thereof may make temporary appointments until the next meeting of the legislature, which shall then fill such vacancies].

No person shall be a Senator who shall not have attained to the age of thirty years, and been nine years a citizen of the United States and who shall not, when elected, be an inhabitant of that state for which he shall be chosen.

The Vice President of the United States shall be President of the Senate, but shall have no vote, unless they be equally divided.

The Senate shall choose their other officers, and also a President pro tempore, in the absence of the Vice President, or when he shall exercise the office of President of the United States.

The Senate shall have the sole power to try all impeachments. When sitting for that purpose, they shall be on oath or affirmation. When the President of the United States is tried, the Chief Justice shall preside: And no person shall be convicted without the concurrence of two thirds of the members present.

Judgment in cases of impeachment shall not extend further than to removal from office, and disqualification to hold and enjoy any office of honor, trust or profit under the United States: but the party convicted shall nevertheless be liable and subject to indictment, trial, judgment and punishment, according to law.

Organization of Congress

Section 4. The times, places and manner of holding elections for Senators and Representatives, shall be prescribed in each state by the legislature thereof; but the Congress may at any time by law make or alter such regulations, [except as to the places of choosing senators].

The Congress shall assemble at least once in every year, [and such meeting shall be on the first Monday in December], unless they shall by law appoint a different day.

Section 5. Each House shall be the judge of the elections, returns and qualifications of its own members, and a majority of each shall constitute a quorum to do business; but a smaller number may adjourn from day to day, and may be authorized to compel the attendance of absent members, in such manner, and under such penalties as each House may provide.

Each House may determine the rules of its proceedings, punish its members for disorderly behavior, and, with the concurrence of two thirds, expel a member.

Each House shall keep a journal of its proceedings, and from time to time publish the same, excepting such parts as may in their judgment require secrecy; and the yeas and nays of the members of either House on any question shall, at the desire of one fifth of those present, be entered on the journal.

Neither House, during the session of Congress, shall, without the consent of the other, adjourn for more than three days, nor to any other place than that in which the two Houses shall be sitting.

Section 6. The Senators and Representatives shall receive a compensation for their services, to be ascertained by law, and paid out of the treasury of the United States. They shall in all cases, except treason, felony and breach of the peace, be privileged from arrest during their attendance at the session of their respective Houses, and in going to and returning from the same; and for any speech or debate in either House, they shall not be questioned in any other place.

No Senator or Representative shall, during the time for which he was elected, be appointed to any civil office under the authority of the United States, which shall have been created, or the emoluments whereof shall have been increased during such time: and no person holding any office under the United States, shall be a member of either House during his continuance in office.

Section 7. All bills for raising revenue shall originate in the House of Representatives; but the Senate may propose or concur with amendments as on other Bills.

Every bill which shall have passed the House of Representatives and the Senate, shall, before it become a law, be presented to the President of the United States; if he approve he shall sign it, but if not he shall return it, with his objections to that House in which it shall have originated, who shall enter the objections at large on their journal, and proceed to reconsider it. If after such reconsideration two thirds of that House shall agree to pass the bill, it shall be sent, together with the objections, to the other House, by which it shall likewise be reconsidered, and if approved by two thirds of that House, it shall become a law. But in all such cases the votes of both Houses shall be determined by yeas and nays, and the names of the persons voting for and against the bill shall be entered on the journal of each House respectively. If any bill shall not be returned by the President within ten days (Sundays excepted) after it shall have been presented to him, the same shall be a law, in like manner as if he had signed it, unless the Congress by their adjournment prevent its return, in which case it shall not be a law.

Every order, resolution, or vote to which the concurrence of the Senate and House of Representatives may be necessary (except on a question of adjournment) shall be presented to the President of the United States; and before the same shall take effect, shall be approved by him, or being disapproved by him, shall be repassed by two thirds of the Senate and House of Representatives, according to the rules and limitations prescribed in the case of a bill.

Powers Granted to Congress
The Congress shall have the power:

Section 8. To lay and collect taxes, duties, imposts and excises, to pay the debts and provide for the common defense and general welfare of the United States; but all duties, imposts and excises shall be uniform throughout the United States;

To borrow money on the credit of the United States;

To regulate commerce with foreign nations, and among the several states, and with the Indian tribes;

To establish a uniform rule of naturalization, and uniform laws on the subject of bankruptcies throughout the United States;

To coin money, regulate the value thereof, and of foreign coin, and fix the standard of weights and measures;

To provide for the punishment of counterfeiting the securities and current coin of the United States;

To establish post offices and post roads;

To promote the progress of science and useful arts, by securing for limited times to authors and inventors the exclusive right to their respective writings and discoveries;

To constitute tribunals inferior to the Supreme Court;

To define and punish piracies and felonies committed on the high seas, and offenses against the law of nations;

To declare war, grant letters of marque and reprisal, and make rules concerning captures on land and water;

To raise and support armies, but no appropriation of money to that use shall be for a longer term than two years;

To provide and maintain a navy;

To make rules for the government and regulation of the land and naval forces;

To provide for calling forth the militia to execute the laws of the union, suppress insurrections and repel invasions;

To provide for organizing, arming, and disciplining, the militia, and for governing such part of them as may be employed in the service of the United States, reserving to the states respectively, the appointment of the officers, and the authority of training the militia according to the discipline prescribed by Congress;

To exercise exclusive legislation in all cases whatsoever, over such District (not exceeding ten miles square) as may, by cession of particular states, and the acceptance of Congress, become the seat of the government of the United States, and to exercise like authority over all places purchased by the consent of the legislature of the state in which the same shall be, for the erection of forts, magazines, arsenals, dockyards, and other needful buildings;—And

To make all laws which shall be necessary and proper for carrying into execution the foregoing powers, and all other powers vested by this Constitution in the government of the United States, or in any depart-ment or officer thereof.

Powers Forbidden to Congress

Section 9. The migration or importation of such persons as any of the states now existing shall think proper to admit, shall not be prohibited by the Congress prior to the year one thousand eight hundred and eight, but a tax or duty may be imposed on such importation, not exceeding ten dollars for each person.

The privilege of the writ of habeas corpus shall not be suspended, unless when in cases of rebellion or invasion the public safety may require it.

No bill of attainder or ex post facto law shall be passed.

No capitation, [or other direct,] tax shall be laid, unless in proportion to the census or enumeration herein before directed to be taken.

No tax or duty shall be laid on articles exported from any state.

No preference shall be given by any regulation of commerce or revenue to the ports of one state over those of another: nor shall vessels bound to, or from, one state, be obliged to enter, clear or pay duties in another.

No money shall be drawn from the treasury, but in consequence of appropriations made by law; and a regular statement and account of receipts and expenditures of all public money shall be published from time to time.

No title of nobility shall be granted by the United States: and no person holding any office of profit or trust under them, shall, without the consent of the Congress, accept of any present, emolument, office, or title, of any kind whatever, from any king, prince, or foreign state.

Powers Forbidden to the States

Section 10. No state shall enter into any treaty, alliance, or confederation; grant letters of marque and reprisal; coin money; emit bills of credit; make anything but gold and silver coin a tender in payment of debts; pass any bill of attainder, ex post facto law, or law impairing the obligation of contracts, or grant any title of nobility.

No state shall, without the consent of the Congress, lay any imposts or duties on imports or exports, except what may be absolutely necessary for executing its inspection laws: and the net produce of all duties and imposts, laid by any state on imports or exports, shall be for the use of the treasury of the United States; and all such laws shall be subject to the revision and control of the Congress.

No state shall, without the consent of Congress, lay any duty of tonnage, keep troops, or ships of war in time of peace, enter into any agreement or compact with another state, or with a foreign power, or engage in war, unless actually invaded, or in such imminent danger as will not admit of delay.

Article II
The Executive Branch

Section 1. The executive power shall be vested in a President of the United States of America. He shall hold his office during the term of four years, and, together with the Vice President, chosen for the same term, be elected, as follows:

Each state shall appoint, in such manner as the legislature thereof may direct, a number of electors, equal to the whole number of Senators and Representatives to which the State may be entitled in the Congress: but no Senator or Representative, or person holding an office of trust or profit under the United States, shall be appointed an elector.

[The electors shall meet in their respective states, and vote by ballot for two persons, of whom one at least shall not be an inhabitant of the same state with themselves. And they shall make a list of all the persons voted for, and of the number of votes for each; which list they shall sign and certify, and transmit sealed to the seat of the government of the United States, directed to the President of the Senate. The President of the Senate shall, in the presence of the Senate and House of Representatives, open all the certificates, and the votes shall then be counted. The person having the greatest number of votes shall be the President, if such number be a majority of the whole number of electors appointed; and if there be more than one who have such majority, and have an equal number of votes, then the House of Representatives shall immediately choose by ballot one of them for President; and if no person have a majority, then from the five highest on the list the said House shall in like manner choose the President. But in choosing the President, the votes shall be taken by States, the representation from each state having one vote; A quorum for this purpose shall consist of a member or members from two thirds of the states, and a majority of all the states shall be necessary to a choice. In every case, after the choice of the President, the person having the greatest number of votes of the electors shall be the Vice President. But if there should remain two or more who have equal votes, the Senate shall choose from them by ballot the Vice President.]

The Congress may determine the time of choosing the electors, and the day on which they shall give their votes; which day shall be the same throughout the United States.

No person except a natural born citizen, or a citizen of the United States, at the time of the adoption of this Constitution, shall be eligible to the office of President; neither shall any person be eligible to that office who shall not have attained to the age of thirty-five years, and been fourteen Years a resident within the United States.

In case of the removal of the President from office, or of his death, resignation, or inability to discharge the powers and duties of the said office, the same shall devolve on the Vice President, and the Congress may by law provide for the case of removal, death, resignation or inability, both of the President and Vice President, declaring what officer shall then act as President, and such officer shall act accordingly, until the disability be removed, or a President shall be elected.

The President shall, at stated times, receive for his services, a compensation, which shall neither be increased nor diminished during the period for which he shall have been elected, and he shall not receive within that period any other emolument from the United States, or any of them.

Before he enter on the execution of his office, he shall take the following oath or affirmation:—"I do solemnly swear (or affirm) that I will faithfully execute the office of President of the United States, and will to the best of my ability, preserve, protect and defend the Constitution of the United States."

Section 2. The President shall be commander-in-chief of the Army and Navy of the United States, and of the militia of the several states, when called into the actual service of the United States; he may require the opinion, in writing, of the principal officer in each of the executive departments, upon any subject relating to the duties of their respective offices, and he shall have power to grant reprieves and pardons for offenses against the United States, except in cases of impeachment.

He shall have power, by and with the advice and consent of the Senate, to make treaties, provided two-thirds of the Senators present concur; and he shall nominate, and by and with the advice and consent of the Senate, shall appoint ambassadors, other public ministers and consuls, judges of the Supreme Court, and all other officers of the United States, whose appointments are not herein otherwise provided for, and which shall be established by law: but the Congress may by law vest the appointment of such inferior officers, as they think proper, in the President alone, in the courts of law, or in the heads of departments.

The President shall have power to fill up all vacancies that may happen during the recess of the Senate, by granting commissions which shall expire at the end of their next session.

Section 3. He shall from time to time give to the Congress information of the state of the union, and recommend to their consideration such measures as he shall judge necessary and expedient; he may, on extraordinary occasions, convene both Houses, or either of them, and in case of disagreement between them, with respect to the time of adjournment, he may adjourn them to such time as he shall think proper; he shall receive ambassadors and other public ministers; he shall take care that the laws be faithfully executed, and shall commission all the officers of the United States.

Section 4. The President, Vice President and all civil officers of the United States, shall be removed from office on impeachment for, and conviction of, treason, bribery, or other high crimes and misdemeanors.

Article III
The Judicial Branch

Section 1. The judicial power of the United States, shall be vested in one Supreme Court, and in such inferior courts as the Congress may from time to time ordain and establish. The judges, both of the supreme and inferior courts, shall hold their offices during good behaviour, and shall, at stated times, receive for their services, a compensation, which shall not be diminished during their continuance in office.

Section 2. The judicial power shall extend to all cases, in law and equity, arising under this Constitution, the laws of the United States, and treaties made, or which shall be made, under their authority;—to all cases affecting ambassadors, other public ministers and consuls;—to all cases of admiralty and maritime jurisdiction, [—to controversies to which the United States shall be a party;—to controversies between two or more states, [between a state and citizens of another state;], between citizens of different states;—between citizens of the same state, claiming lands under grants of different states, and between a state, or the citizens thereof, and foreign states, [citizens or subjects].

In all cases affecting ambassadors, other public ministers and consuls, and those in which a state shall be party, the Supreme Court shall have original jurisdiction. In all the other cases before mentioned, the Supreme Court shall have appellate jurisdiction, both as to law and fact, with such exceptions, and under such regulations as the Congress shall make.

The trial of all crimes, except in cases of impeach-ment, shall be by jury; and such trial shall be held in the state where the said crimes shall have been committed; but when not committed within any state, the trial shall be at such place or places as the Congress may by law have directed.

Section 3. Treason against the United States, shall consist only in levying war against them, or in adhering to their enemies, giving them aid and comfort. No person shall be convicted of treason unless on the testimony of two witnesses to the same overt act, or on confession in open court.

The Congress shall have power to declare the punishment of treason, but no attainder of treason shall work corruption of blood, or forfeiture except during the life of the person attainted.

Article IV
Relation of the States to Each Other

Section 1. Full faith and credit shall be given in each state to the public acts, records, and judicial proceedings of every other state. And the Congress may by general laws prescribe the manner in which such acts, records, and proceedings shall be proved, and the effect thereof.

Section 2. The citizens of each state shall be entitled to all privileges and immunities of citizens in the several states.

person charged in any state with treason, felony, or other crime, who shall flee from justice, and be found in another state, shall on demand of the executive authority of the state from which he fled, be delivered up, to be removed to the state having jurisdiction of the crime.

[No person held to service or labor in one state, under the laws thereof, escaping into another, shall, in consequence of any law or regulation therein, be discharged from such service or labor, but shall be delivered up on claim of the party to whom such service or labor may be due.]

Federal-State Relations

Section 3. New states may be admitted by the Congress into this Union; but no new states shall be formed or erected within the jurisdiction of any other state, nor any state be formed by the junction of two or more states, without the consent of the legislatures of the states concerned, as well as of the Congress.

The Congress shall have power to dispose of and make all needful rules and regulations respecting the territory or other property belonging to the United States; and nothing in this Constitution shall be so construed as to prejudice any claims of the United States, or of any particular state.

Section 4. The United States shall guarantee to every state in this union a republican form of government, and shall protect each of them against invasion; and on application of the legislature, or of the executive (when the legislature cannot be convened) against domestic violence.

Article V
Amending the Constitution

The Congress, whenever two thirds of both houses shall deem it necessary, shall propose amendments to this Constitution, or, on the application of the legislatures of two thirds of the several states, shall call a convention for proposing amendments, which, in either case, shall be valid to all intents and purposes, as part of this Constitution, when ratified by the legislatures of three fourths of the several states, or by conventions in three fourths thereof, as the one or the other mode of ratification may be proposed by the Congress; provided [that no amendment which may be made prior to the year one thousand eight hundred and eight shall in any manner affect the first and fourth clauses in the ninth section of the first article; and] that no state, without its consent, shall be deprived of its equal suffrage in the Senate.

Article VI
National Debts

All debts contracted and engagements entered into, before the adoption of this Constitution, shall be as valid against the United States under this Constitution, as under the Confederation.

Supremacy of the National Government

This Constitution, and the laws of the United States which shall be made in pursuance thereof; and all treaties made, or which shall be made, under the authority of the United States, shall be the supreme law of the land; and the judges in every state shall be bound thereby, anything in the constitution or laws of any State to the contrary notwithstanding.

The senators and representatives before mentioned, and the members of the several state legislatures, and all executive and judicial officers, both of the United States and of the several states, shall be bound by oath or affirmation, to support this Constitution; but no religious test shall ever be required as a qualification to any office or public trust under the United States.

Article VII
Ratifying the Constitution

The ratification of the conventions of nine states, shall be sufficient for the establishment of this Constitution between the states so ratifying the same.

Done in convention by the unanimous consent of the states present the seventeenth day of September in the year of our Lord one thousand seven hundred and eighty seven and of the independence of the United States of America the twelfth. In witness whereof we have hereunto subscribed our Names.

Bill of Rights

Amendment I.

Congress shall make no law respecting an establishment of religion, or prohibiting the free exercise thereof; or abridging the freedom of speech, or of the press; or the right of the people peaceably to assemble, and to petition the Government for a redress of grievances.

Amendment II.

A well regulated Militia, being necessary to the security of a free State, the right of the people to keep and bear Arms, shall not be infringed.

Amendment III.

No Soldier shall, in time of peace be quartered in any house, without the consent of the Owner, nor in time of war, but in a manner to be prescribed by law.

Amendment IV.

The right of the people to be secure in their persons, houses, papers, and effects, against unreasonable searches and seizures, shall not be violated, and no Warrants shall issue, but upon probable cause, supported by Oath or affirmation, and particularly describing the place to be searched, and the persons or things to be seized.

Amendment V.

No person shall be held to answer for a capital, or otherwise infamous crime, unless on a presentment or indictment of a Grand Jury, except in cases arising in the land or naval forces, or in the Militia, when in actual service in time of War or public danger; nor shall any person be subject for the same offence to be twice put in jeopardy of life or limb; nor shall be compelled in any criminal case to be a witness against himself, nor be deprived of life, liberty, or property, without due process of law; nor shall private property be taken for public use, without just compensation.

Amendment VI.

In all criminal prosecutions, the accused shall enjoy the right to a speedy and public trial, by an impartial jury of the State and district wherein the crime shall have been committed, which district shall have been previously ascertained by law, and to be informed of the nature and cause of the accusation; to be confronted with the witnesses against him; to have compulsory process for obtaining witnesses in his favor, and to have the Assistance of Counsel for his defence.

Amendment VII.

In Suits at common law, where the value in controversy shall exceed twenty dollars, the right of trial by jury shall be preserved, and no fact tried by a jury, shall be otherwise re-examined in any Court of the United States, than according to the rules of the common law.

Amendment VIII.

Excessive bail shall not be required, nor excessive fines imposed, nor cruel and unusual punishments inflicted.

Amendment IX.

The enumeration in the Constitution, of certain rights, shall not be construed to deny or disparage others retained by the people.

Amendment X.

The powers not delegated to the United States by the Constitution, nor prohibited by it to the States, are reserved to the States respectively, or to the people.

Report Links

The Internet sites described below can be accessed at
http://www.myreportlinks.com

▶**The National Archives Experience: Bill of Rights**
Editor's Choice See and search important documents from the formative years of American history.

▶**Rights of Citizens: The Bill of Rights**
Editor's Choice The Bill of Rights explained in terms young people can understand.

▶**Documents From the Continental Congress and the Constitutional Convention, 1774–1789**
Editor's Choice Get a feel for how ideas were expressed at the Constitutional Convention.

▶**Liberty! The American Revolution**
Editor's Choice Study the events surrounding the American Revolution.

▶**The James Madison Center: Bill of Rights**
Editor's Choice Find out how James Madison proposed the Bill of Rights.

▶**U.S. Constitution: Amendments to the Constitution of the United States of America**
Editor's Choice Read the text of the Bill of Rights. Annotations make it easier to understand.

▶**American Civil Liberties Union**
Learn about the views and activities of a group devoted to protecting individual rights.

▶**American Civil Liberties Union: Student Rights**
See efforts to ensure that students are protected by the Bill of Rights.

▶**Americans United for Separation of Church and State**
Read the views of a controversial group that seeks to preserve religious freedom.

▶**Anti-Defamation League: Religion in the Public Schools**
What is the proper role of religion in public education? This site provides legal points of view.

▶**The Anti-Federalist Papers**
Anti-Federalists were wary of the proposed Constitution. Find out why.

▶**Article 19: Global Campaign for Free Expression**
Get a global outlook on issues of freedom of speech.

▶**Brady Campaign to Prevent Gun Violence**
The Brady Campaign gives voice to those who wish to limit gun use.

▶**Capital Punishment (Multnomah County Library Homework Center)**
Get started in understanding the debate over capital punishment in the United States.

▶**Citizens Flag Alliance**
Learn the views of those who want to keep people from being able to burn flags.

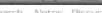
Report Links

The Internet sites described below can be accessed at
http://www.myreportlinks.com

▶**Electronic Privacy Information Center**
Browse articles about the modern-day handling of privacy rights issues.

▶**Exploring Constitutional Conflicts**
See both sides of the issue in the flag burning controversy.

▶*The Federalist:* **A Collection of Essays**
Read The Federalist Papers, which were important to the development of the Constitution.

▶**First Amendment Center**
Learn about the history of the First Amendment, and its importance in modern times.

▶**Gunston Hall Plantation**
Visit the home of George Mason, the "Father of the Bill of Rights."

▶**Historical Documents: The Magna Carta**
The Magna Carta is a British document that influenced the development of the Bill of Rights.

▶**Human Rights Watch**
Read about an effort to protect human rights throughout the world.

▶**Miranda Law: A Guide to the Privilege Against Self-Incrimination**
Find out the importance of the Miranda warning.

▶**National Rifle Association**
Learn about the NRA's efforts to support gun owners and the Second Amendment.

▶**The Nobel Peace Prize 1991**
Aung San Suu Kyi won the 1991 Nobel Peace Prize. Read her acceptance speech.

▶**Reporters Without Borders for Press Freedom**
Freedom of the press is easy to take for granted. Read about global efforts to fight censorship.

▶**Rise of Parliament: Making History**
The English Bill of Rights is a document that influenced the United States' Bill of Rights.

▶**U.S. Constitution: Fifth Amendment**
Get a better understanding of the Fifth Amendment and the concept of due process.

▶**The White House: James Madison**
Read about the life of President James Madison, who submitted the Bill of Rights for approval.

▶**The White House: Thomas Jefferson**
Learn about the life of Thomas Jefferson, statesman and president.

amend—Make a change; make something better.

appeal—A challenge of a decision made by a court, by seeking to have the case decided in another court.

ambush—Jump out from a hiding spot and attack.

assemble—Meet together in a group.

bail—Money held by a court; it allows a person to go free until his or her trial.

censor—Stop something from being published.

colonist—A person who lives in a colony.

colony—A settlement of people far from their home country.

Constitution—The rules and laws that govern the way a nation works.

constitutional—In accordance with the U.S. Constitution.

convention—A formal meeting of people.

democracy—A government ruled by the people.

draft—Require a citizen to serve in the United States military.

espionage—The act of spying to give secret information to another country.

Exclusionary Rule—Courts must throw out evidence police got from an illegal search.

Federalist—A supporter of the federal government set up by the Constitution.

fine—Money that is required to be paid out as a form of punishment.

imminent—About to happen.

incite—Urge into action.

incriminate—Give testimony that shows someone is guilty of a crime.

justice—A judge who sits on the U.S. Supreme Court.

libel—Words that are not truthful and make a person look bad.

minor—A person under the age of eighteen.

pamphlet—A piece of paper with information.

petition—Formally ask for something in writing.

prior restraint—Stop something before it happens.

racketeer—A dishonest person out to make money; a cheat.

ratify—Agree to make into law.

redress—Make amends for; set right.

warrant—A document from a judge that gives police the power to search.

Chapter 1. The Sacred Rights of Humanity

1. Leonard W. Levy, *Origins of the Bill of Rights* (New Haven, Conn.: Yale University Press, 2001), pp. 3–4.

2. Reporters Without Borders, "Worldwide Press Freedom Index 2005," *Reporters Without Borders for Press Freedom,* n.d., <http://www.rsf.org/rubrique.php3?id_rubrique=554> (July 14, 2006).

3. Reporters Without Borders, "Akbar Ganji Freed," *Reporters Without Borders for Press Freedom,* n.d., <http://www.rsf.org/print.php3?id_article=16795> (June 16, 2006).

4. President George W. Bush, "Statement on a Call for the Unconditional Release of Akbar Ganji in Iran," *The White House, Office of the Press Secretary,* July 12, 2005, <http://www.whitehouse.gov/news/releases/2005/07/2005071 2-5.html>, (July 14, 2006).

5. Radio Free Europe/ Radio Liberty, "Apostasy Case Reveals Constitutional Contradictions," *RFE/RL Afghanistan Report, vol. 5, no. 9,* April 3, 2006, <http://www.rferl.org/reports/aspfiles/printonly.asp?po=y> (June 22, 2006).

6. Radio Free Europe/ Radio Liberty, "Convert Flees, Ripples Continue," *RFE/RL Afghanistan Report, vol.5, no.10,* April 15, 2006, <http://www.rferl.org/reports/afghan-report/2006/04/10-15046.asp> (June 11, 2006).

7. Clark Boyd, "The Price Paid for Blogging Iran," *BBC World News,* February 21, 2005, <http://news.bbc.co.uk/go/pr/fr/-/11/hi/technology/4283231.stm > (June 18, 2006).

8. Reporters Without Borders, "Jailed Blogger

Taken to Sit University Exams in Handcuffs," *Reporters Without Borders for Press Freedom,* January 24, 2006, <http://www.rsf.org/print .php3?id_article=16242> (June 11, 2006).

9. BBC News, "Profile: Aung San Suu Kyi," *BBC World News,* May 25, 2006 <http://news .bbc.co.uk/go/pr/fr/-/1/hi/world/asia-pacific/1950505.stm> (June 23, 2006).

10. Simon Montlake, "Burma's Black Friday," *BBC World News,* June 16, 2003, <http://news .bbc.co.uk/go/pr/fr/-/1/hi/world/asia-pacific/2993196.stm> (July 21, 2006).

11. The Website of Dau Aung San Suu Kyi, "Paul McCartney and Eric Clapton record CD to help Burmese Activist," *Dau Aung San Suu Kyi's Pages,* September 27, 2004, <http://www.dassk.org /announcements.php> (June 11, 2006).

12. Letter to Thomas Jefferson, October 17, 1788, Saul K. Padover, ed., *The Complete Madison* (New York: Harper & Brothers Publishers, 1953), p. 254.

Chapter 2. America:
Land of the Free

1. Thomas Jefferson et al., "Declaration of Independence," *The U.S. National Archives and Records Administration,* July 4, 1776, <http: //www.archives.gov/national-archives-experience /charters/declaration.htm> (July 21, 2006).

2. Leonard W. Levy, *Origins of the Bill of Rights* (New Haven, Conn.: Yale University Press, 2001), p. 2.

3. John R. Vile, *A Companion to the United States Constitution and Its Amendments, Third Edition* (Westport, Conn.: Praeger, 2001), p. 6.

4. Richard Morris, *The Framing of the Federal Constitution* (Washington, D.C.: Department of the Interior, 1986), p. 50.

5. Ibid., pp. 80–81.

6. Levy, p. 26.

7. Donald A. Ritchie, *Our Constitution* (New York: Oxford University Press, 2006), p. 15.

Chapter 3. Understanding the Bill of Rights

1. Ellen Alderman and Caroline Kennedy, *In Our Defense: The Bill of Rights in Action* (New York: William Morrow and Company, Inc., 1991), p. 13.

2. John R. Vile, *A Companion to the United States Constitution and Its Amendments, Third Edition* (Westport, Conn.: Praeger, 2001), p. 129.

3. Roger Williams, The Ship Letter 1654 or 1655 as quoted in Francis Graham Lee, ed. *Church State Relations* (Westport, Conn.: Greenwood Press, 2002), p. 28–29.

4. *Schenk* v. *United States,* 249 U.S. 47, 52 (1919).

5. Brady Campaign to Stop Handgun Violence. "Firearm Facts," *Brady Campaign to Stop Handgun Violence,* June 2005, <www.bradycampaign.org /facts/factsheets/pdf/firearm_facts.pdf> (July 21, 2006).

Chapter 4. Defending Freedom— The Bill of Rights at Work

1. *Schenck* v. *United States,* 249 U.S. 47 (1919).

2. *Chaplinsky* v. *New Hampshire,* 315 U.S. 568 (1942).

3. *R.A.V.* v. *St. Paul,* 505 U.S. 377 (1992).

4. *Texas* v. *Johnson,* 491 U.S. 397 (1989).

5. *United States* v. *Eichman,* et al., 496 U.S 310 (1990).

6. *Edwards* v. *South Carolina,* 372 U.S. 229 (1963).

7. *The New York Times* v. *Sullivan,* 376 U.S. 254 (1964).

8. Thomas L. Tedford and Dale A. Herbeck, *Freedom of Speech in the United States* (State College, Penn.: Strata Publishing, Inc., 2001), p. 225.

9. *Engel* v. *Vitale,* 370 U.S. 421 (1962).

10. *Abington Township* v. *Schempp,* 374 U.S. 203 (1963).

11. *U.S.* v. *Miller,* 307 U.S. 174 (1939).

Chapter 5. The Supreme Court Upholds the Constitution

1. *Weeks* v. *United States,* 232 U.S. 383 (1914).

2. *Mapp* v. *Ohio,* 367 U.S. 643 (1961).

3. Leonard W. Levy, *Origins of the Bill of Rights* (New Haven, Conn.: Yale University Press, 2001), p. 196.

4. *Miranda* v. *Arizona,* 384 U.S. 486 (1966).

5. *Lucas* v. *South Carolina Coastal Council,* 505 U.S. 1003 (1992).

6. *Doggett* v. *United States,* 505 U.S. 647 (1992).

7. *Gideon* v. *Wainwright,* 372 U.S. 335, (1963).

8. Anti Death Penalty.org, "Bureau of Justice Statistics on the Death Penalty," *Anti Death Penalty Website,* March 2006, <www.antideathpenalty.org/statistics.html> (July 21, 2006).

9. *Furman* v. *Georgia,* 408, U.S. 238 (1972).

10. *Thompson* v. *Oklahoma,* 487 U.S. 815 (1988).

11. *Griswold* v. *Connecticut,* 381 U.S. 479 (1965).

12. *Loving* v. *Virginia,* 388 U.S. 1 (1967).

Chapter 6. Living in America: Recent Debate About the Bill of Rights

1. *Reno* v. *American Civil Liberties Union,* 521 U.S. 844 (1997).

2. Ibid.

3. *Tinker* v. *Des Moines Independent Community School District,* 393 U.S. 503 (1969).

4. Ibid.

5. *Hazelwood School District* v. *Kuhlmeier,* 484 U.S. 260 (1988).

6. *New Jersey* v. *T.L.O.,* 469 U.S. 325 (1985).

7. *Vernonia School District 47J* v. *Acton,* 515 U.S. 646 (1995).

8. *Lee* v. *Weisman,* 505 U.S. 577 (1992).

9. *Santa Fe Independent School District* v. *Doe,* 530 U.S. 290 (2000).

Berry, Joy Wilt. *Mine and Yours: Human Rights for Kids*. New York: PowerHouse Books, 2005.

Bramwell, Neil D. *James Madison*. Berkeley Heights, N.J.: MyReportLinks.com Books, 2003.

DK Publishing. *Eyewitness Books: The American Revolution*. New York: Doris Kinderling Publishing, 2005.

Freedman, Russell. *In Defense of Liberty: The Story of America's Bill of Rights*. New York: Holiday House, 2003.

Friedman, Ian C. *Freedom of Speech and the Press*. New York: Facts On File, 2005.

Giddens-White, Bryon. *The Supreme Court and the Judicial Branch*. Portsmouth, N.H.: Heinemann, 2005.

Haesly, Richard, ed. *The Constitutional Convention*. San Diego, Calif.: Greenhaven Press, 2002.

Hudson, David L. *The Bill of Rights: The First Ten Amendments of the Constitution*. Berkeley Heights, N.J.: Enslow Publishers, Inc., 2002.

January, Brendan. *The Supreme Court*. New York: Watts Library, 2004.

Justice Learning. *The United States Constitution: What It Says, What It Means: A Hip Pocket Guide*. New York: Oxford University Press, 2005.

Rivera, Sheila. *The Bill of Rights*. Edina, Minn.: Abdo and Daughters Publishing, 2004.

Yero, Judith Lloyd. *American Documents: The Bill of Rights*. Washington, D.C.: National Geographic Children's Books, 2006.

A

ACLU, Reno v., 94–96
Action, Vernonia School District 47J v., 103–104
"Address and Reasons of Dissent of the Minority of the Convention," 36
Afghanistan, 13
American Library Association, United States v., 96–97
Anti-Federalists, 35–37, 40
Arizona, Miranda v., 80–82
Articles of Confederation, 5, 28–30
athletes, drug testing of, 103–104

B

Bill of Rights
  about, 7–9
  adoption of, England, 5, 28
  adoption of, U.S., 5, 37–40
  enforcement of, 19–21
  text of, 115
Burma, 16–19
Bush, George H. W., 66, 105
Bush, George W., 12

C

Chaplinsky v. New Hampshire, 61
Children's Internet Protection Act, 96–97
City of St. Paul, R.A.V. v., 61–65

civil trials, 54–55, 87, 115
Communications Decency Act, 95–96
Connecticut, Griswold v., 91
the Constitution
  authority of, 58
  ratification of, 5, 35–37
  state, 27–28
  text of, 108–115
  writing of, 5, 30–32
cruel & unusual punishment, 57, 87–91, 115

D

death penalty, 6, 51, 87–91
Declaration of Independence, 5, 22
Des Moines Independent Community School District, Tinker v., 97–99
Doggett v. United States, 84–86
double jeopardy, 52
drug testing, 103–104

E

Edwards v. South Carolina, 67–69
Eighth Amendment, 55–57, 87–91, 115
eminent domain, 53, 82–84
Engel v. Vitale, 73
Espionage Act, 6, 59–60
Exclusionary Rule, 80
executive branch, 32

F

Federalists, 35–37
Fifth Amendment, 51–53, 80–84, 91, 115
fighting words, 45, 61
First Amendment, 40–47, 91, 97–101, 105, 115
flag burning, 6, 65–67
Flag Protection Act, 6, 67
Flag Protection Amendment, 6, 67
Fourteenth Amendment, 5, 76–77, 91–92
Fourth Amendment, 49–51, 101–103, 115
freedom of assembly and petition, 45, 67–69
freedom of religion
  conversion and, 12–13
  history of, 23, 42–43
freedom of speech
  described, 43–45
  fighting words, 45, 61
  flag burning and, 6, 65–67
  hate speech, 61–65
  history of, 9–12
  on the Internet, 14–16, 94–97
  libel, 69–72
  U.S. Supreme Court on, 6, 44–45, 61, 64, 97–99
freedom of the press, 45–47, 99–101
freedom to other rights, 57–58, 115

Furman v. *Georgia*, 89

G
Ganji, Akbar, 10–12
Georgia, Furman v., 89
Gideon v. *Wainwright*, 86–87
Griswold v. *Connecticut*, 91
gun control, 6, 48, 74–76
Gun-Free School Zones Act, 6

H
hate speech, 61–65
Hazelwood School District v. *Kuhlmeier*, 99–101
Holmes, Oliver Wendell, 44–45
Human Rights Watch, 15–16

I
the Internet, freedom of speech on, 14–16, 94–97
interracial marriage, 6, 91–92
Iran, 9–10, 14–16

J
Jefferson, Thomas, 5, 34–35
Johnson, Texas v., 65–67
judicial branch, 32

K
King, Martin Luther Jr., 69–72
Kuhlmeier, Hazelwood School District v., 99–101

L
Lee v. *Weisman*, 104–105
legislative branch, 31

libel, 69–72
Loving v. *Virginia*, 91–92
Lucas v. *South Carolina Coastal Council*, 82–84

M
Madison, James, 5, 20, 33–35, 37–40, 77
Magna Carta, 5, 28
marriage, interracial, 6, 91–92
Mason, George, 5, 32, 40
Miller, United States v., 74–75
Miranda v. *Arizona*, 80–82
Myanmar, 16–19

N
National Firearms Act, 74–75
New Hampshire, Chaplinsky v., 61
New Jersey v. *T.L.O.*, 101–103
Ninth Amendment, 57–58, 115
Nobel Peace Prize, 17, 18
no excessive bails/fines, 55–57, 115

O
Objections to the Constitution, 5
Oklahoma, Thompson v., 90

P
prayer in public schools, 6, 73, 104–105
presumption of innocence, 52–53
prior restraint, 72–73

privacy rights, 49–51, 91, 101–104, 115
public schools. *See* schools.
Puritans, 5, 43

Q
Quartering Act, 49

R
Rahman, Abdul, 13
R.A.V. v. *City of St. Paul*, 61–65
Reno v. *ACLU*, 94–96
Reporters Without Borders, 9, 10
Revolutionary War, 26–27
right to a fair and speedy trial, 53, 84–86, 115
right to a jury of one's peers, 53–55, 87, 115
right to a public trial, 53, 115
right to bear arms, 47–48, 74–76, 115
right to counsel, 53, 86–87, 115
right to due process, 51–53, 115
right to face accuser, 53–54, 115
Roper v. *Simmons*, 90–91
rule by force, 16–19

S
Saminejad, Mojtaba, 15–16
Schenck v. *United States*, 6, 59–60
schools
freedom of the press in, 99–101
free speech in, 6, 97–99

prayer in, 6, 73,
104–105
privacy rights in,
101–104
student's rights
in, 97
search & seizure,
49–51, 80,
101–103, 115
Second Amendment,
47–48, 74–76, 115
Sedition Act, 60
self incrimination,
protection against,
52–53, 80–82
separation of church
and state, 43, 73
Seventh Amendment,
54–55, 87, 115
Simmons, Roper v.,
90–91
Sixth Amendment,
53–54, 84–87, 115
soldiers, quartering,
48–49, 115
South Carolina,
Edwards v., 67–69
South Carolina Coastal
Council, Lucas v.,
82–84
states, powers held by,
56–58, 115
Sullivan, The New York
Times v., 69–72
Suu Kyi, Aung San,
16–19

T
taxation, 26, 51
Tenth Amendment,
56–58, 115
Texas v. Johnson,
65–67
The Federalist Papers,
5, 35–36

The New York Times v.
Sullivan, 69–72
The New York Times v.
United States,
72–73
Third Amendment,
48–49, 91, 115
Thompson v.
Oklahoma, 90
Tinker v. Des Moines
Independent
Community School
District, 97–99
T.L.O., New Jersey v.,
101–103
Twenty-seventh
Amendment, 40

U
United States
government, branches
of, 31–32
history of, 22–27
United States, Doggett
v., 84–86
United States, Schenck
v., 6, 59–60
United States, The New
York Times v.,
72–73
United States, Weeks
v., 80
United States v.
American Library
Association, 96–97
United States v. Miller,
74–75
unreasonable search &
seizure, 49–51, 80,
101–103, 115
U.S. Supreme Court
on the death
penalty, 6, 89–91
described, 21, 32
on Espionage Act,
6, 59–60

on flag burning, 6,
65–67
on freedom of
assembly, 67–69
on free speech, 6,
44–45, 61, 64,
97–99
on gun control, 6,
74–76
on interracial mar-
riage, 6, 91–92
justices, photograph
of, 20
on prayer, 6, 73,
104–105

V
Vernonia School District
47J v. Action,
103–104
Virginia, Loving v.,
91–92
Virginia Declaration of
Rights, 5, 32
Vitale, Engel v., 73

W
Wainwright, Gideon v.,
86–87
Washington,
George, 37
Weeks v. United
States, 80
Weisman, Lee v.,
104–105
Williams, Roger, 43
World War I, 5–6,
59–60